"Mary Elizabeth's captivating stories demonstrate through real-life challenges that our capacity to lead can lie dormant until we're forced to take a stand or to survive. Our world is calling us to lead wherever we are, and this book is a potent reminder of the innate capacity and power that each of us hold to change the world."

Gail Larsen
Founder of Real Speaking®, Author of *Transformational Speaking: If You Want to Change the World, Tell Better Story* www.realspeaking.com

"Mary Elizabeth has written a truly remarkable book about how life experiences can translate into leadership capabilities. She insists on how each one of us has immense power behind us. When called upon with intention, this power brings action beyond our wildest imagination. This important book will help bring awareness on how to unmask your hidden power and bring it into the world."

Patt Lind-Kyle
Author: "Heal Your Mind, Rewire Your Brain" and "When Sleeping Beauty Wakes Up" www.pattlindkyle.com

"Mary Elizabeth Young's brilliant leadership comes from the kind of experience that needs a BIG VOICE in the world. She leads from her inner authority, not authority over others. She is centered in the primal, intuitive knowledge that includes things men wouldn't dream of. Most importantly, none of this is "mental." Her experience is one of transcending her own self-negation and rising to the occasion of her life and visions in some of the most extraordinary ways I have ever seen. **Read this book**. It will give you what YOU need to be a woman who is leading in her own life."

Bill Lamond
Creator of Fulfillment-based Living, Author of "Born to Lead" www.billlamond.com

"Mary Elizabeth's natural genius is as a leader with women, not in the old masculine paradigm but one of truly "juicing" women to see and bring forth their gifts to the planet. This is simply who Mary Elizabeth is and how she lives her life. She is the feminine principle going forth in action. I have constantly received the blessings of her wisdom, compassion and deep seeing. I am thrilled that she has written this incredible book that comes from the depth of her own life experiences to touch, inspire, and move women all over the world to tap into their own innate wisdom and rise at this exciting time on our planet!"
Kathleen Plant McIntire
Author and creator of Guiding Signs 101 Intuition cards, www.SoaringInLight and www.GuidingSigns101.com

"As a leader and an author, Mary Elizabeth Young powerfully calls us forth as women to dream big and step into our dreams to take the lead in creating a world that works for all."
Robin Milam
Administrative Director, Global Alliance for the Rights of Nature; global advocate, One World Awake www.OneWorldAwake.org

"I have the honor of saying that I have been a witness to Mary Elizabeth's life for the past 18 years, and have known many of these stories in real time. Her book is a living testimonial of the possibility when you are willing to accept your life as a gift that fine tunes and hones the soul. She is a demonstration of a fully dimensional life of reflection and examination from which we can learn and integrate lessons. She has stepped into her

wisdom years with a desire to awaken these strengths in other women. She is a leader from the feminine model."
Marilyn Nyborg
Co-Founder, Past President of Gather the Women Global Matrix, Founder of Women Waking the World www.womenwakingtheworld.com

"For over twenty years I've watched Mary Elizabeth coach and empower so many women to live fully, lead powerfully, and fulfill their dreams—including me! Read this book and join us in co-creating a world that works for everyone!"
Gracie MacKenzie
Wild Wise Woman, author, and New Thought singer-songwriter
www.blogher.com/wild-alien-mystic

"Life's challenges contain gifts that train us to be leaders. Mary Elizabeth inspires us to take the gifts and lead us to a brighter future for all."
Elisa Parker
Co-founder of See Jane Do, activist and visionary for women, co-creator of "Passion into Action", www.seejanedo.com

"If the art of living is the ability to use misfortune in a constructive fashion, Mary Elizabeth Young's latest book, "Wise and Ready to Rise" has provided a superb example of how this is to be accomplished. A helpful and inspirational book, I will share it with many of my personal and professional friends."
Cynthia Stewart
Author of *"Dream Big, Creating Wealth on the Web"* and founder of NetLinked Solutions.www.CynthiaStewart.com

Wise and *Ready* to Rise

Ten Powerful Ways
Life Teaches Us to Lead

Mary Elizabeth Young

San Diego, California

Copyright @ 2013 by Mary Elizabeth Young

All rights reserved. No part of this book may be reproduced or transmitted in any form or by any means, electrical or mechanical, including photocopying, recording or any information storage and retrieval system, without written permission from the publisher.

For information:
Mary Elizabeth Young
www.WiseAndReadyToRise.com

Cover Design by Ellen Frudakis and Erin Cote-Kinsey

ISBN **978-0-9891680-0-7**

Printed in the United States of America

First Edition, August 2013

For my mother and daughters,
who taught me how to lead,
and for Betsy Donovan,
who told me, I had a book to write.

Note to the Reader

I invite you to read this book from your own perspective, spiritually speaking.

Whatever name you give to Spirit, or if you have a different set of beliefs altogether, please substitute this name or belief in its place whenever I mention it throughout this book.

Contents

Acknowledgements ii

Introduction – Life prepares us for leadership and women are neede now to lead on all levels vi

Part One ~ We are Guided by Spirit to Wisdom and Leadership 1

Chapter One 3

> First Message: Everything happens in life for a reason. Seek the deeper meaning and this wisdom will sustain you through challenges and bring you to your greatest joy. You will inspire others to do the same.

Chapter Two 13

> Second Message: You are not alone. Seen and unseen forces are at work helping you every step of the way, lighting your path. You also light the path for others.

Chapter Three 31

> Third Message: Listen to your intuition. Your example teaches others to do the same.

Part Two ~ Find the Gifts in Challenges 41

Chapter Four 43

> Message Four: Feel your feelings from the challenges you face. This will open your heart and expand your capacity for compassion, courage, and extraordinary leadership.

Chapter Five 57

> Message Five: Open up to all the good that wants to come your way and your vision becomes realized.

Chapter Six 73

> Message Six: Even in the midst of chaos and confusion, stay grounded. Your strength assists others to find their own.

Chapter Seven 91

> Message Seven: Allow what you cannot change to transform you so that you become the person you were meant to be.

Part Three ~ Shine Your Leadership Light and Make an Impact 107

Chapter Eight 109

> Message Eight: Keep Moving Forward With Inspired Action

Chapter Nine 119

> Message Nine: Find Clarity, Set Intentions and Attract Miracles

Chapter Ten 129

> Message Ten: Believe in yourself and your dreams

Chapter Eleven 137

> Love the Challenges: Give Gratitude and Appreciation for Everything and THRIVE!

About the Author 151

*If ever there comes a time
when the women of the world come together
purely and simply for the benefit of mankind,
it will be a force such as the world has never known."
– Matthew Arnold*

Acknowledgements

Getting this book written and into print has taken a whole team of amazing talent and love.

This book started as an idea in the 1980's when writing letters was the traditional form of communication. I met a woman named Betsy Donovan in New England and cared for her mother, Elizabeth, who was diagnosed with Alzheimer's disease. We became true "Sistahs" during that time and kept in touch by letters when I came back to California. She complemented my writing and often encouraged me to write a book. She also succumbed to Alzheimer's, so Betsy, wherever you are now, this book is for you.

As you read the story of my daughter getting lost in a cave in Chapter Two, you will discover it was such an amazing story that I had to write it. Diane Covington, a writing teacher and coach, helped me submit it to a magazine for print. When that didn't happen, it sat on the back burner. Betsy's reminder "You have a book to write" kept nudging me;

I brought up the idea of writing a book to my Mastermind/Heart Triad group with Robin Milam and Kathleen McIntire. As you'll read in Chapter Ten, we changed the name of our group from Mastermind to Heart Triad to match our feminine leadership calling. When I mentioned the book idea, we all took a writing class together. They have been my ongoing book "birth" coaches and have done brainstorming, peer review, editing, website building, and cheer-leading of the highest order to this endeavor. On top of that, they are the dearest "heart sister friends".

When my daughter, Kyra, was lost in the Catacomb Cave at the Lava Beds National Park on her fifth grade field trip along with a classmate, you'll read how many people it took to find them. I would publicly like to thank the staff and parents of the Nevada City School of the Arts, the rangers and staff of the Lava Beds National Park, the Siskiyou Sherriff Search and Rescue and dog team, Dr. Bill Broeckel, Jim and Liz Wolff, Vern Clift, Russell Yoder and the members of the Shasta Area Grotto of the National Speleological Society, all the volunteers who supported the search effort and cooked us dinner, KVMR (the local radio station who kept the community informed), all the people who were praying for or offered good will for the safe return of the children and for all of the unseen forces at work, please know I will be forever grateful to you. I also want to thank Kyra for being willing to share this powerful story of keeping hope alive that has such a miraculous heart-warming ending.

As I kept searching for a theme to write a book about, my writing mentors kept telling me to write about other stories in my life. Since I had written about Kyra, I started writing about my experiences with my older daughter, Ellen. I am deeply grateful to her for being willing to share her story of experiencing bipolar disorder. My hope is that it will help many parents and children who have experienced this and ultimately, how mental illness can be a gift.

At one point, the book was going to have an inspirational focus assisting those going through difficult circumstances in overcoming challenges. I wrote the stories about my late husband, Bob Bolender (AKA Robert Young) and his experience with colon cancer.

Ultimately, it was my coach and "brother" Bill Lamond, who read the manuscript and asked me why I wasn't writing a book about women's leadership. I had to wonder myself as I had devoted 20 years to being an activist for this. I was thrilled to finally have a direction, and one that I loved. What leader doesn't face a challenge? I realized that all of these stories from my life taught me how to be a leader. Our world needs more women leaders. I completed the book with the intention that it will have women claim their natural leadership skills that life has taught them, just as mine has. Thank you, Bill.

Where does one first learn how to be a leader?

For most of us, it is our parents. As a woman, our first teacher of feminine leadership is our mother, if we are blessed enough to have one. I have been fortunate to have such a loving and courageous mother, Virginia Crabb. It wasn't always easy for her to step up and lead, but she did it anyways. Thanks for doing that, Mom, and for being an inspiration for this book.

Thanks to my family, those related by both blood and acquired through our heart connection: Tom Crabb, Doug Crabb, Terry Crabb, and their families, Hilary Herman, Walter Mahoney, Mathieu Young, Chris Young, Damon, Jennifer Young Harris and family, Dorothy Donaldson and family, Ron Kidder, and all who have loved and encouraged me through this process. I also send deepest gratitude to my dad, L. Leigh Crabb, who was my biggest supporter and always believed in me. I know you are still with me, leading from your heart and inspiring me in spirit, Dad, to do the same.

CiCi Stewart, a published author, truth-sayer, and the dearest of friends, gave me honest advice from her own experience to help me find my authentic voice. Our frequent conversations bolstered my spirit and self-confidence. Your friendship means the world to me.

My best friend, Gracie MacKenzie, was always there to cheer me through the blocks and doubts. Thank you, Gracie, for sharing your love and your courageous story in this book. You were by my side through most of the stories in this book and I thank you with all my heart for your love and sisterhood.

My Gather the Women "Spokes" including Marilyn Nyborg, Judith Hurley Prosser, Angie Lux, and Nancy Naumann as well as Elisa Parker of See Jane Do were all a source of never ending encouragement.

Writing the book is one thing, but getting it into a read-able format is another. My dearest thanks go to all who helped along the way starting with Patricia Dove Miller and my writing class buddies, Heather Donahue and Shirley Dickhard. You gave me the belief that I had some stories to share. Christine Kloser and the Transformational Author's Experience and Contest nudged me further. Thank you, Molly Fisk, for your wisdom and assisting me ready Kyra's cave story for the Transformational Author's Contest and ultimately win an editing prize. Betsy Graziani Fasbinder brought me a new way of seeing how I could position my stories and keep moving forward. Marlene Oulton, Clifford, Todd, Janet Wind and Donald Prothero were the final editors and I bow to you in deep gratitude and appreciation.

To anyone I have erroneously omitted, please accept my deepest thanks as for whatever you did to bring this book to form, as it wouldn't have happened without you!

May every author be so blessed to have this foundation of support from which to create their writing. I will never be the same thanks to this experience of writing this book and how each of you contributed to it.

Introduction

"The reason for all challenges, Mary Elizabeth, is so that you can finally learn that none are bigger than you."
—*The Universe*

When life changes dramatically for us, sometimes in an instant, we are faced with going deep inside ourselves to find a way to make it through the challenge. The intensity of the challenge demands that we find a powerful response that can transform us to become more of who we came into this life to be… if we allow it.

This is a book about leadership and how challenges re-veal our guidance skills. It is a book that anyone can learn from, but the truth is, I have written it specifically for women. I believe the problems our world is facing are calling for us to enhance our natural leadership skills. If you are a man reading this, I hope this book speaks to you and can teach you how to develop additional skills that bring wholeness and fulfillment to your life. Please, share it with the women in your life.

For twenty years I've known that women's leadership is the key to creating the world that we all want for ourselves, our families, and for generations to come. This world is one in which there are enough basic necessities for everyone; an environment where all have the opportunity to live fulfilling lives; where conflict can be negotiated through collaboration, and where we can co-exist in harmony with nature and help the earth and its creatures heal from years of using more resources than were sustainable. Even though I've been a leader for most of my life in schools, family, business, com-munity, and in the world, and could be a leader in creating the world I envisioned, something almost always held me back.

Maybe you feel the same way.

A variety of reasons would scroll through my head every time I felt a nudge to really step up. That voice would seductively point out that I didn't have enough "letters" after my name to qualify as a true leader. It would remind me that my high school English teachers had screamed at me for my atrocious writing, so I could never author a book. It pointed out my long list of failures, reminding me that I had to put others first, especially my family, as their needs and successes were more important than mine. That voice was right. I couldn't and wouldn't lead.

But through all the twists and turns of my life's journey, something was shaping me to be the real leader I always wanted to be. I kept moving forward and dreaming. I kept preparing myself. Even when I look back on the times I thought I wasn't a leader, I was.

I knew deep inside there was an even a bigger role for me to play in my life. I knew I was to call everyday women out of their comfort zones to become more engaged in leading and creating the kind of world that works for all, in harmony with nature.

The truth is all it takes is to raise your hand, open your mouth, and say "I'll be the lead on that"; to take the stand that something important to you shall be realized. My mother says it so well: "I was always afraid to be the leader, but the truth is, once I did it, I found it was so easy. I just had to make sure everyone I was leading was doing their job." That is one way to lead. Others find leadership in a co-creative collaborative model through partnership and teams where everyone holds accountability for the end result. The main thing is, leadership can happen in an instant, and you, as a woman, are totally prepared for it, whether you realize it or not.

My mother found that her place to express leadership was locally through the PTA, Girl Scouts, and the YWCA. She says my being a good student inspired her to engage herself in doing more with her life. As the PTA President and Girl Scout Leader, she taught me my first leadership lessons. We were a tag team from my earliest years. It's true: mothers and daughters naturally teach each other how to express our innate talents for leadership.

With all the advances in women's rights and opportunities to create lives of our own choosing, there are so many ways that women can live satisfying lives. There are now more women in college than men, more women were employed during the recent recession than men, and research data proves when leadership teams have a minimum of 30% women involved, the creativity, innovation, and overall results of the organization are improved. „The magic number became known as the 30% solution, the idea being that once women reached a Critical Mass in an organization, people would stop seeing them as women and start evaluating their work as managers. Harvard Academic, Rosabeth Moss Kanter, originally developed this theory more than 40 years ago in her book *"Men and Women of the Corporation."*

Still, we haven't reached parity in wages or top leader-ship positions in business, government, or organizations. In fact, the percentage of women in leadership roles has stayed steady at 18% for decades, and on average we make 77 cents for every dollar a man makes.[12] Only 33 of the Fortune 1000 companies are headed by women. Our not standing up for women's value in the marketplace and in leadership positions doesn't just hurt us; the world our children and future generations are inheriting has less opportunity for them too. What's the real result? Its humanity's overusing the earth's environmental and financial resources. We can change this. In 2011 a strengths-based research study by Zenger and Folkman, took a sampling of 7,280 male and female leaders from progressive, successful companies, and they were rated by their peers, bosses, direct reports, and other associates. Women on an overall leadership effectiveness index were rated significantly more positively than males. Joe Folkman, President, noted: "While men excel in the technical and strategic arenas, women clearly have the advantage in the extremely important areas of people relationships and communication. They also surpass their male counterparts in driving for results."[3]

Fortunately, women are increasingly taking their skills and using them in starting their own businesses. Between 1997 and 2007 the number of women-owned businesses grew 40% faster than those owned by men. In 2007, 7.8 mil-lion businesses were owned by women, accounting for 30% of the non-farm, privately held US firms. In spite of this, women-owned businesses only account for 11% of the sales and 13% of the employees among privately held companies.

These businesses average 25% of the sales receipts of men-owned firms. The annual earnings ratio between female and male owned businesses is only 55%, much lower than the salary ratios in non-self-employed men and women. Women entrepreneurs enjoy the autonomy of owning their own businesses, but not yet the financial parity with men. The brightest spot for economic growth during the last decade is the fact that women-owned businesses created jobs when larger privately held firms were losing them.⁴ I sense that we are building momentum.

I learned twenty years ago how valuable our contributions are to solving the enormous social justice issues like world hunger, poverty, and violence against women. I attended the United Nations Conference on Women in Beijing, China, in 1995 with my family, where the First Lady of the United States, Hilary Rodham Clinton, declared that "Women's Rights are Human Rights and Human Rights are Women's Rights." I was inspired to come back to my rural Nevada County community in Northern California and share what I learned from this experience. Meeting together with like-minded women, we created a women's leadership coalition. This planted the seeds for the success of a movement named "Gather the Women" which held annual yearly events on International Women's Day that spark the leadership light in the women attendees. "Gather the Women of Nevada County" was formed as a result of Gather the Women Global Matrix, which established local regions to carry out the vision of the original model. Forty communities like ours in the United States, Canada, and Europe hold events every year, reminding women that we are the key to creating a world that works for all. Today women come together in circles locally to grow and expand themselves throughout the year.

Over the years our community has become more conscious. Town hall meetings were held on the local meth addiction crisis and human trafficking. Activism blossomed in the community as well, from locally grown food awareness, homelessness support, and animal rescue, alternative education for children, protecting the environment, and living sustainably. The consciousness of our small foothill community was rising and much of the area was thriving. More women's empowerment energies blossomed; separate from GTW, including a local radio and multimedia program called See Jane Doe and a yearly women's event called Passion into Action. I committed to completing this book during their 2011 conference.

Yet in this last decade, with all of the good so created, the world still seemed to be on a path of social and environmental degradation. I attended the Marianne Williamson Sister Giant weekend in 2012 where she spoke about the difficulties our children face. Even in America in 2011, 16.1 million or approximately 22% of children in the US lived in poverty.[5] Twenty percent[6] or more of children in 36 states lived in food insecure households in 2010. The District of Columbia (30.75%) and Oregon (29%) had the highest rates of children in households without consistent access to food.[7]

While the War on Drugs was instituted by President Richard Nixon as a way to curb drug addiction, building prisons still takes precedence over constructing buildings for higher education. Over the past 23 years, California constructed roughly one new prison per year, at a cost of $100 million dollars each, while building only one new public college during the same period. Nationwide, **spending on prisons has risen six times faster than spending on higher education**. We imprison more people than any other country one earth, including China, which has four times our population.[8]

Our children on the whole are not getting the education necessary to prepare them to live successfully and care for themselves and their families. Global warming is bringing us monster storms, rising oceans, and species disappearing every day. The overall message: we are not going to sustain life on earth unless we make big and lasting changes… soon.

The challenge is here. The world is calling to us, and it is calling us to lead NOW. Many have already answered this call. As Paul Hawken stated in his commencement address[2009] for the University of Portland, Oregon, "... for the first time in history a group of people organized themselves to help people they would never know, from whom they would never receive direct or indirect benefit. And today tens of millions of people do this every day. It is called the world of non-profits, civil society, schools, social entrepreneurship, non-governmental organizations, and companies who place social and environmental justice at the top of their strategic goals. The scope and scale of this effort is unparalleled in history." There are men and women heeding the call and many of you are most likely part of this movement. The message now is to bring more people along, and to especially encourage more women to step up and raise their hands.

We have never been more prepared to answer this call. We have everything it takes to do what is needed. Every day, in developing countries where resources are scarce, women take on the responsibility of ensuring that their families are fed; have potable water, clothing, housing, healthcare, and education, plus regular meaningful celebrations and spiritual connections. In the developed world where we have so much more opportunity and material goods, we too, do what is needed for our families and communities, and can also naturally take the lead to bring our world to a place of thriving.

The challenges in my life have contributed to expanding my natural leadership capabilities. I offer them in this book to assist you on your path to leadership expression. The stories I share here prepared me for this moment, and for every moment in the future where I will raise my hand and take the lead. You have lived your experiences and they too, have primed you for this time. There is a reason you are here on the earth. Your specific gifts and talents as a leader are needed.

We have a unique calling to lead. Maybe it is within your household, neighbourhood, community, or perhaps you are being called to lead on a national or global stage. You know inside you what this expression is; that spark of leadership that yearns for you to make your unique impact on this world. Each chapter in this book shares a message that I was given from the challenges I faced. These messages taught me something powerful, bringing me more feminine wisdom and the confidence to step into leadership. My intention is that this book will assist you to step into yours.

Challenges beg us to grow. Humanity and our world are facing enormous ones. We have the opportunity to expand our awareness of them, see how we are called to respond with our natural leadership, and use our gifts and talents to create a better world for all.

We are wise and ready to rise!

Mary Elizabeth Young

NOTES

1. Nicki Gilmour, Why Accountability is What Matters: Achieving Critical Mass with Targets or Quotas, January 21, 2010
2. http:www.aauw.org/learn/research/uploads/simpletruthaboutpaygap1.pdf
3. http://www.zfco.com/media/articles/ZFCo.WP.WomenBetterThanMen.031312.pdf
4. Taken from Why Accountability is What Matters: Achieving Critical Mass with Targets or Quotas.
5. http://feedingamerica.org/hunger-in-america/hunger-facts/child-hunger-facts.aspx#sthash.7H4T98Xh.pdf
6. http://www.esa.doc.gov/sites/default/files/reports/documents/women-owned-businesses.pdf
7. Gundersen, C., Waxman, E., Engelhard, E., Del Vecchio, T, Satoh, A.& Lopez-Betanzos, A. (2012).Map the Meal Gap 2012: Child Food Insecurity. Feeding America.
8. Bloom, Lisa, When will the U.S. stop mass incarceration? Special to CNN updated 12:21 PM EDT, Tue July 3, 2012
9. http://www.dominican.edu/dominicannews/study-backs-up-strate-gies-for-achieving-goal

Part One

~

We are Guided by Spirit to Wisdom and Leadership

Chapter One

"And once the storm is over, you won't remember how you made it through, how you managed to survive. You won't even be sure, whether the storm is really over. But one thing is certain. When you come out of the storm, you won't be the same person who walked in. That's what this storm's all about.
-Haruki Murakami

**First Message:
Everything happens in life for a reason.
Seek the deeper meaning and this wisdom will sustain you through challenges and bring you to your greatest joy.
You will inspire others to do the same.**

Everyone has them–defining moments. These are times when we are tested beyond our abilities; times when something overpowers us physically, emotionally, psychically, or spiritually, like an act of nature, a health crisis, or a loss that seems too great to bear.

In these moments energy awakens in us to make it through the crisis. Whatever the outcome, success or loss, we are forever changed, especially when we see these moments as a part of our path that teaches us something. How you view what happens in your life will change the course of it.

Will you allow each incident, no matter what the outcome, to enlighten you, to lead you to become more of who you came here to be? Or will it define you as a victim of fate, powerless to make sense of what happens in your life?

The choices you make and the decisions you make during these critical moments define your life. Do you choose to live or die, tell the truth or lie, go along with the crowd, or stand up for what you believe? Do you take the lead or keep quiet and hope someone else does? Sometimes we don't even experience an event as a defining moment until later. That was the case for me. My first defining moment happened when I was eight years old.

"Watch out for your sister", Mom yelled, as we left the rented San Clemente beach house, the screen door slamming behind us.

My two older brothers and I walked the few blocks to the golden sands of a Southern California beach that wasn't crowded for an August day, even though it was the height of vacation season. Still, my brothers wanted to climb over the fence to an adjoining abandoned private beach. The challenge of swimming without a lifeguard probably lured them to this deserted stretch of sand. Wanting to be as good at anything my brothers did, I followed right behind.

I wore my favorite two-piece red bathing suit and was eager to get in the water and swim. I breathed in the salty ocean air mixed with the Coppertone suntan lotion my mom had rubbed on my back and shoulders. This was my 8th summer and Doug and Tom were 10 and 12 years of age. They wore their Hawaiian white flower print swimming trunks with solid color backgrounds, with a white waistband and trim along the leg hems. Toms were blue and Doug's were red.

The crashing waves looked enticing as I laid my rainbow colored beach towel down on the sand. The ocean was a grey/blue color; the sky overcast with moisture that usually burned off later in the morning. I couldn't wait to get in the water to ride the waves and feel their powerful churning energy propelling me forward.

This beach didn't have the canvas air mattresses we liked to rent up the coast at Huntington Beach. In San Clemente, it was body surfing or nothing. We waded into the water together. I loved the way the waves hurled my body fast over the smooth water surface below. Mimicking my brothers until I got it right, I flew over the water. The waves crashed, pushing us backwards and then suddenly the current would change as the tide pulled the water into the next wave, tugging us forward with it. The surf was strong that day. We were riding the waves together until I noticed I was further out than my brothers. I watched them walk onto the beach and lie down on their towels.

I'll just ride a few more waves and then come in and rest.

Big waves didn't scare me. Earlier, I watched my brother's dive under big waves, so I followed their lead. I came up on the backsides unscathed and felt like a porpoise. My brothers started to look like dots on the sand and there weren't many waves out where I was.

I guess I need to start swimming in so I can catch more waves.

Swimming had always been a part of summer. My mom got us into swimming as toddlers. Nearly every day we went to the neighborhood "Plunge" or drove to the beach from our home in Glendale. We liked swimming in open water. This day; I felt secure. But my strong crawl stroke wasn't getting me any closer to shore. I swam harder and harder, finally getting some lift from the wave swells, but they pushed me backwards, not forwards to the beach. This was so different. I was getting tired.

A chill ran over my forehead and down my neck as I was pulled out to sea. Fear stabbed me in my chest. I was alone, far from the beach, getting out of breath. I swam harder to get into the wave pattern. Suddenly the waves swelled. One caught me at its crest, hurling me down hard onto the smooth grey green base of the ocean. I was caught underwater for a long time before its rolling power loosened its grip and popped me to the surface, gasping for a breath. I wished my brothers were out here to give me a tug into shore. I yelled for them, but they were too far away to hear me. They lay motionless on their towels, unmoved by my cry for help.

I lost my focus as another massive wave crashed on top of me. I felt like I was in a giant washing machine being tossed around and around, not knowing which way led to the surface. I was pummeled by the pounding ocean, not able to set myself up to ride the energy of a wave into shore. I kept trying to touch bottom, to grip my toes into the sand and force my body towards the safety of my towel and brothers.

I barely got a breath before another giant wave crashed on top of me, knocking the breath out of my lungs, and throwing me down hard on the sandy bottom, grinding me around and around, down in the sandy soup-like bottom, tearing at my skin like sandpaper. I was completely disoriented, but somehow I kept clawing my way up to the surface, for breath, for life. I was losing energy and air, when the thought came to me that I was drowning. "Come up for air", a voice called to me.

I didn't know where "up" was. I was in a liquid coffin of white, frothy, salty bubbles and sand, flopping around with flustered, convulsive, ineffective strokes, like a baby bird that had been dropped out of its nest into a huge puddle of water.

The voice and its energy commanded me, "DO NOT GIVE UP NOW. THIS IS NOT THE WAY YOUR LIFE IS GOING TO END. KEEP FIGHTING! KEEP SWIMMING! YOU CAN DO THIS! YOU WILL DO THIS!

I extended my last bit of strength and air as I clamored to the surface, gasped and sucked in a huge breath.

"KEEP GOING UNTIL YOU CAN TOUCH THE BOTTOM", the voice cheered me on. This time my toes grabbed the sandy ocean floor and I pushed myself hard against the strong current, aching for precious air. I had never swum in such deep, powerful waves.

Out of nowhere, a surge of water pushed me towards the shore. The balls of my feet and then the entire soles were able to grab the bottom and help me lumber towards safety. My legs, strong from bike riding, running, climbing trees, and doing everything to keep up with my brothers, were weak, shaky, and stinging like needles. I was getting closer to shore, but was weary from the pounding of the monster waves on my body that I desperately needed a hand. I tried to yell for help, but only a hoarse, weak bark came out. My brothers lay limp on their towels while the beating waves pounded like baseball bats on enormous bass drums, drowning out my cries for help.

Finally, I crumpled in a heap on my towel. Near tears, I told my brothers that I had almost drowned. They lifted their heads up, grinned at each other, and snickered sinisterly-"Please. Don't tease me now. I need your love and a welcome-back-from-near-death hug," I wanted to say; I didn't dare cry or they would roar with laughter. I turned my head and silently wept; drowning in lonely sorrow.

"They really didn't care if I died out there," I thought. It was quiet for a long time.

After I gathered some strength, I walked to our cottage, slowly following my brothers who had decided to go back for lunch. I hadn't let the waves pull me under and I wasn't going to let their behavior stop me from enjoying my vacation.

Later that evening as our family walked to a restaurant for dinner I told my parents what happened. My brothers were walking further ahead.

I got caught in the waves today and couldn't come up for air" I said timidly to my mom and dad.

"Oh my God! What happened?" Mom asked. My stomach and heart cramped up into tight balls and my throat tightened.

"I was out swimming alone."

"Alone?" my Mother gasped, "Why were you alone?" I cringed, slowly admitting what happened, but was relieved she wanted to hear my story alone, instead of bringing my brothers into it for a three-way interrogation.

"We climbed over a fence to a beach that wasn't open. There was no lifeguard."

"You went into the water alone? I've told you never to do that, Mary Beth!"

"I know. At first we went into the water together and rode the waves. Tom and Doug got out, but I wanted to stay in longer. They were lying on the beach and they were too far away."

"Why were you swimming so far away?"

"The tide pulled me way out. The big waves pounded me down. I felt like I was in a washing machine and couldn't come up for air. I was so scared. I thought I was going to drown!" I sputtered. Tears fell down my cheeks. My Mom put her arm around me and comforted me.

"I'm so sorry this happened," my dad said in a soft, low, tender voice into my ear from behind me.

"How did you ever get out of the water?" Mom asked.

"I fought hard to come up and get a breath. I kept trying to touch the bottom so I could stand and pull myself out. Finally when I was so tired and my legs ached and ached, I felt the sand under my toes and started pulling myself out."

"Didn't Tom and Doug help you?"

"I yelled for them, but they were lying on their towels and didn't hear me."

"Oh my gosh!" Mom said.

"When I got to my towel I was so tired and my legs were shaking. I fell down on the beach and told Tom and Doug I almost drowned."

I swallowed hard as more tears came and my throat felt like needles were sticking in it.

"They laughed at me" I choked. Sadness flooded through me.

"Oh, dear, dear", my Mom said as she squeezed me. My parents heard my words and understood how horrific the experience was for me. My dad yelled for my brothers to stop walking. They turned around slowly.

"What happened today on the beach?" he asked them. They looked down at their feet and avoided looking at him.

"I dunno," they mumbled in chorus.

"Your sister just told us she almost drowned and that you didn't help her." "We didn't see anything," came their reply.

"I know, she told us. You weren't watching out for her, were you?"

"I guess not," one of them said after a long silence.

"She said you laughed at her when she told you what happened, that she almost drowned," Dad said sternly.

They kept their heads bowed in silence. Everyone was holding his or her breath.

"We. don't treat people like that in this family," my Mom exclaimed!

More silence. I hid behind my parents.

"Tell your sister you're sorry," Mom said.

Still looking down, they mumbled, "Sorry."

"Okay, then. I don't EVER want this to happen AGAIN."

No swimming alone and no more being mean to one another. Do you hear me?" Mom warned.

My brothers and I looked down at our feet and mumbled yes in unison. We slowly walked on to dinner.

As a child, I could only think of how lucky I was to survive that moment when I could have drowned. It takes only twenty to sixty seconds. With more strength than I knew I had and inspiration from a higher power, I was able to pull myself up for air and keep moving closer to shore, digging my toes into the sand, and stopping the tide from pulling me back out to sea.

As an adult, I realized the deeper significance of this experience. When my first daughter was in elementary school, we were asked at a Parent/Teacher night to view all major events in a child's life from the perspective that they teach them lessons beneficial to their growth and development. This caused me to remember my near drowning experience. Why had this happened to me? What was the lesson? Was there something beneficial that I gained from it besides knowing not to swim alone?

I believe my near drowning was the defining moment where my life became worth fighting for—that I could make it through any challenge, be wiser, have more courage, and be able to draw on my strength and my higher power no matter how great the event. This gift happened when I was eight.

At age thirty as I began this journey in leadership, I had no idea what challenges I would face. But one thing was clear. Remembering the near drowning left me no longer a victim of this incident, but enriched by it. I started looking at the challenging times I'd experienced as events that contained gifts, such as my first pregnancy that ended in a miscarriage contained a gift of compassion for me and all women who experienced this tragedy. When I divorced at a young age and became a single mom of a toddler; I learned to sustain a family on my own. When my ex-husband didn't participate in our daughter's life, I learned how to let go of expectations, to forgive him, and speak positively to our daughter about her father, no matter how he participated in our lives. The grief and loss from these experiences deepened me and gave me a knowing that I was creating a deep well within my soul that could be filled not just with sorrow, but with the sweetest gift of grief ~Joy.

Looking for the deeper meaning in challenges tempers you for leadership and prepares you to seek wisdom in other difficult challenges.

Chapter Two

"The cave you fear to enter holds the treasure you seek."
-Joseph Campbell

Second Message:
You are not alone.
Seen and unseen forces are at work helping
you every step of the way, lighting your path.
You also light the path for others.

By the time my second daughter, Kyra, reached the age of eleven, I had a lot of experience being a single parent. Eight years had been spent raising her older sister, Ellen, after my first marriage ended in divorce. Two more years I had solo-parented Kyra, as her father, Bob, my second husband, had died two years earlier. Single or not, parenting is a leadership role. You'd think being the breadwinner, cook, shopper, chauffeur, nurse, recreational and financial manager would train me to able to keep track of my daughter and her friend on a school field trip. This, however, offered a new challenge when I chaperoned a field trip for Kyra's fifth grade class exploring caves at the Lava Beds National Monument in Northern California.

I called, but they didn't answer.

"Kyra…Kai…" I yelled.

Silence.

Where are they? They said they would be right here. I should know better. They are both so rambunctious they've probably wandered off. Now what should I do?

A third child I was chaperoning, Emily, and I had walked out of this last cave we were exploring because I needed to take a "nature" break, plus it was getting close to dinner time. Emily was looking back towards the entrance to the cave when I came out from behind the bushes.

"Aren't they here yet?" I said, annoyed with the delay. "Well, I guess we'd better go back in and get them."

Emily looked scared, but I just figured something got the other kids attention and they were taking their time coming out.

Why did everything look different as we retraced our steps? For a brief second, a slight chill went up my back and neck. It was dark and cramped where this meandering lava tube was narrowing, and I had to bend down in order to navigate through the cave. Even with the flashlight on, I couldn't remember these lava formations from when we walked in the first time.

I had let each of the three children choose one cave to explore. We had already seen the caves that Kyra and Emily had chosen. Kai had chosen this Catacomb cave, and even though it was getting late, we headed in so he could have his turn. Kyra was heading in to explore without a jacket, but I had insisted she grab one of mine.

Each of the caves had unique characteristics, but most was like being in big, dark rooms. Some had large charcoal-colored lava encrusted tunnels that appeared on the side that you could walk through and wound back to the open room. The deeper you walked into a cavern, the ceiling came flowing down to meet the floor. This was our signal to turn around and head back out.

I'd heard a parent rave about a cave where they discovered a glorious display of stalagmites and stalactites. I told the three kids how fun it would be to find this magical cave room.

When we first headed into Kai's cave I knew right away it was different. It didn't have the one "big room." It had four tunnels that eerily greeted us when we walked in. I felt drawn to the tunnel on the right and said, "Let's go this way." There wasn't a flat path to walk on. This small tunnel was darker than the 'big room' tunnels we had been exploring, so we had to depend on flashlights to show us the way. We found big globs of lava that hung down from the ceiling or pushed up from the floor—some the size of tractor tires. We had to duck, bend, twist our bodies, and lift our legs up, over, and around these lava boulders to navigate through the cave. We passed by huge open 'windows' in the tunnel that revealed other tunnels branching off from the one we were in. One would need ropes and ladders to reach the bottom of these caverns. We kept moving until it became too difficult for me to continue, as the ceiling was too low, obstructed with lava globs. Plus, as I mentioned before, nature was calling and I really had to go.

"Come on, kids. It's time to go back out.

"It seemed I had been saying that phrase all afternoon. Our routine at the end of a cave was for me to call out, "Time to go back out," and we'd turn around and walk out together. Emily was by my side, but Kyra and Kai said, "We'll be right there." They were laughing and having a great time. I felt everything was fine, and they would follow right be-hind us. They were both eleven, and would start middle school soon.

They didn't come out.

Emily and I went back in, yelling for Kyra and Kai. We were a tight team of four while. Exploring the caves all afternoon. It had been a fun bonding experience. I now felt the void of their absence and wanted Kyra and Kai back now.

Everything looked different. The air smelled stale and lifeless. I couldn't tell if this was the spot where I had seen them last. I got a sick feeling in the pit of my stomach that something was wrong and knew immediately I had to get help to find them.

Emily and I hustled out of the cave and flagged down Lori, another chaperone, who had stopped by with a station wagon full of giggly girls. Their voices hushed when they heard we couldn't find Kyra and Kai.

Everyone piled out of the car and headed into the cave to help me search for them. I heard gasps from the girls as we entered. It suddenly hit me that this was an enormous and tricky cave, with the four tunnels at the entrance and a maze of others that opened off from them. If Kyra and Kai were lost, how would we ever find them?

We kept yelling their names, but didn't even bother wriggling our bodies through the bulging lava tunnel we had gone down before as this cave now felt too ominous and complicated. We needed expert help to find these children. Why didn't I realize this and turn around when we had first walked in? I told Lori that I would call the Ranger Station. She took her charges and Emily, and said she would tell Steve, Kyra and Kai's teacher, what had happened.

Being the youngest and always trying to be as strong and brave as my brothers, a cave with four tunnels didn't scare me when we'd first entered, but now I questioned my bravado.

I called the Ranger Station after 5:00 pm. A woman's voice said, "Oh, the kids may be lost now, but eventually they will find their way out. I will let the Rangers know."

She sounded like this happened often and if she wasn't concerned, I needn't worry either. Just in case, I called my friend Sarah who suggested we call Silent Unity, a twenty-four hour prayer line, and ask for prayers that the children would come out safely and soon.

Come on, Kyra and Kai. Please don't take too long.

At 5:30 pm, Steve and three male chaperones arrived at the cave. They had that *"We're going to go in there and find those kids now!"* kind of attitude in their steps, like an army platoon on a mission.

I was feeling embarrassed and guilty that I hadn't paid closer attention to where Kyra and Kai were as I was walking out of the cave. Why hadn't I just turned around and made sure they were walking behind me? Weary from three days traveling and having a physical need tugging at my senses, my awareness antennae weren't on full alert. I wished I hadn't encouraged the search for the magical cave room.

This third time in as I showed Steve and the other dads where I had last seen the kids, the cave seemed even less familiar. I was beginning to realize how easy it would be to get lost in this cave. The men climbed down through a large opening to the left where the brown spiky rock bottom tunnel extended out of sight. I sat with a dad who decided to wait with me until the others would come back with the kids. There was a damp chill in the air. Water drops splat-tired on the dried lava and us. The dank smell of wet earth permeated the dark tunnel. It felt cold and scary as the minutes dragged on. Soon we stood up and walked out of the cave. I was imagining what Kyra and Kai were feeling. They must be scared and cold, too.

After more than an hour of waiting, the men returned.

Breathless and worn-out, defeat etched in the lines on Steve's forehead and fear infusing his words, he admitted they couldn't find them.

His fear unnerved me. Why had the woman at the Ranger Station said the children would eventually come out?

Where are they? Why couldn't the men find them? They had a map of the cave and everything. *"How could I have walked out of the cave without them?"* I asked myself over and over.

Where are the Rangers anyways? It was 8:00 pm. We called an emergency number. The voice said they would find the on-call Ranger and have him come find the children.

"What? Wasn't my earlier phone call about missing children serious enough?"

A group of concerned parent chaperones now waited with me. A couple, Barb and Dave, had parked their RV by the cave to give us a warmer place to congregate.

At 10:00 pm two Rangers arrived. The older one with curly grey/brown hair and a mustache did his best to re-live my fears.

"I think I know where they are. It will take me about thirty minutes to get into the loop area in the back of the cave that a lot of people get lost in. I'll have them out as soon as I can."

I felt hopeful, thanks to his positive attitude and the authority of his experience. I prepared myself to welcome the kids back, get them dinner, and tuck them into their sleeping bags. Everyone else had been wondering why it had taken the Rangers so long to get there, but I was just glad they had arrived and knew what to do.

An hour ticked by…then another. We took turns sitting around the small booth table in the RV. What do you say at a time like this? There was a lot of nervous chatter. Questions were asked about how this had happened, with everyone being careful not to imply anyone was at fault. People were jokingly saying that if anyone would get lost in a cave, it would be Kyra and Kai, the mischievous ones. No one wanted to face the possibility that these children were irretrievably lost, hurt, or even worse. It was too soon to think that, but a whisper was creeping into my thoughts.

After midnight the Rangers came out and the look on the chief Ranger's face was unmistakable. These big, strong, experienced men who always found the lost people had come back without our kids. Fear infused their beings, too. Now they wondered if Kai and Kyra had wandered out of the cave and been kidnapped.

That was a bizarre thought. We had stood by the only pathway that led to the cave since just after 5:00 pm, seven hours earlier. Now that it was looking like the children had vanished, this bizarre possibility had to be considered too. "We're calling in the Siskiyou County Sheriff's Search and Rescue, but they won't be here until morning. We'll continue to hold vigil and search the surrounding area."

Someone said they would call Kai's parents. I flinched when I thought of receiving a call saying your child is lost in a cave.

My stomach was in knots as I took everything in. A voice in my head was saying, *"This can't be happening. This is all a bad dream. I am going to wake up soon."* My mind was trying to protect me from too much to contemplate.

Barb and Dave kindly offered me the bedroom in the back of their RV. It was a windy night and the sagey, dusty smells emanating from the desert landscape around the caves leaked into the RV. I huddled in the back listening to men yelling out Kyra and Kai's names all night long. I was safe and warm inside the motor home, but where were the children? A low rumble of panic vibrated through my body keeping me from sleep. I prayed to Spirit and the angels to keep Kyra and Kai safe. I didn't plead because that would validate how seriously scared I was, although I was beginning to feel that way. My mind volleyed another perspective that this too was all a dream so I didn't really need to worry.

I coped by silently thinking "Oh boy!" like you would shout out when going over too big of a rapid on a raft trip, hanging on to the sides of the boat to keep from falling overboard. *"Oh boy!"* kept repeating itself. I felt like I was being whipped around on a carnival ride that was too scary, yet not revealing how frightened I was because someone might laugh at me. *"Oh boy!"* limited this experience to something bearable.

Heavy sighs let out the anxiety that was too much to keep inside. They felt like high-pressured air coming out of an overinflated bike tire.

One moment I was relieved that I had made Kyra put on my jacket. The next moment I worried if their flashlights were still working. I imagined them cold, damp, and really frightened. I shook.

Why did we go in that cave? Catacombs meant a place where the dead were buried. Early Christians were buried in Catacombs, a place of meandering tunnels where people often got lost. My mind cycled back and forth between my grief over being so thoughtless, the children being alone, lost, and hungry in the cave or perhaps being with some stranger if the kidnapping theory was a reality. Through those long hours of waiting, I felt every bit of fuzz on the maroon blanket I had pulled around me. The Ranger's truck had a bright light shining from it that seemed to interrogate me all night long, "Why did you allow them to go into this cave?"

At 5:00 am the senior Ranger knocked on the door of the RV and told me to meet the Captain at the Visitor's Center at 6:00 am. A little before then I got in my car and headed out. It felt strange to be getting in the car alone and driving back to the Visitor's Center. Still dark outside, I walked up to the Center. A Ranger escorted me into a small room with a table and a few chairs.

Keep in mind that I had strived to be a "good" girl growing up, got mostly A's in school, trying to be a good citizen by serving on jury duty, voting in elections, and paying my taxes. I regularly tithed to organizations that helped to end world hunger and improve the environment, and here I was volunteering for my daughter's school. Yet somehow this situation felt like I was being led to the principal's office or worse, a firing squad. I just had no experience being this far in the wrong or in such a predicament. As a nurse, I was used to helping people and relieving suffering, not causing it.

I sat down across from a freshly shaven uniformed man. Captain Tom Miller was engraved on a gold nameplate pinned to his shirt. I think I had brushed my hair, hadn't I? As the lead Ranger Officer in charge of this National Park, he asked me to tell him what had happened. At one point he asked the dreaded question, "Why did you walk out of the cave without the children?"

My emotions flooded out as I answered his questions. I asked myself again how I could have walked out without them. I sobbed from the sadness, shame, and guilt I had been holding inside. I told Captain Miller I had not meant to leave without them.

"I thought they were right behind me."

I should have made sure they were following yet I had to pee. It was a mistake, probably the biggest one of my life. None of my reasons seemed good enough. I had lost my husband a few years earlier to cancer. Was I now going to lose my daughter? Would I be responsible for someone else's child dying?

The Captain squinted his eyes, with a rigid neck and his arms and hands folded tightly across his chest, even his body was shaming me. He told me he was sending the Search and Rescue Unit, including search dogs, into the cave. Because of the first Ranger's idea that the children could have been kidnapped, he was considering issuing an Amber Alert, a statewide alert on radio, TV, and highway signage that children had been abducted. His stern attitude and humiliating tone let me know he was not happy with me. I hate not making people happy.

I also sensed the financial and human resource burdens of the search effort. Every hour the children were lost weighed even heavier on Captain Miller's shoulders. He had closed the National Park for the day due to the search efforts, which added to his dilemma.

"I need some of the children's clothes so the dogs can get their scent. Underwear is the best because it carries the strongest scent."

I wiped my eyes, blurted out thanks for his help, and left to retrieve the clothing.

As a mother, you make sure your kids have enough clean underwear packed when they go on a trip. It was surreal to go in search of Kyra and Kai's dirty underwear. The knots twisted tighter in my stomach.

Back at the original campsite, everyone was finishing breakfast and packing to leave. Parents and students stared in an awkward silence as I walked in. Before this trip I had been a school board member, closely involved in the inner workings of this charter school. This morning I felt like an outcast. Angry looks forced me to grab Kyra and Kai's underclothing and head back to the Captain.

Around 8:00 am the Search and Rescue team and dogs arrived. Not long after, Kai's father, Tim, drove up in his red Jeep Wrangler. His eyes looked tense and tired from driving all night, but his body looked ready to leap into action. I welcomed him and explained what the Sheriff and Rangers were doing. I was relieved when he didn't harangue me for losing his son in a cave, and with unspoken compassion, he became my ally.

He wanted to go in the cave and search with the team, but they wouldn't let him. Yellow tape was going up all around the area surrounding the cave. The Rangers closed Lava Beds National Park for the day. Kai and Kyra had now been lost for 15 hours. I felt hopeful that the search team would bring them out.

An hour went by... then another.

This situation wasn't looking or feeling good. It was mid-morning now and the sky was grey and overcast. My nerves were wearing thin and I needed more support. I called my mom from a phone at the Visitor's Center. I sobbed when I told her Kyra was lost in the cave. I was beginning to face a parent's worst fear, that of losing a child, maybe forever. Kyra's teacher saw me crying and gave me a hug. I called my sister, Hilary. She and her husband, Walter, were driving to Chico from the San Francisco Bay Area to go to her best friend's memorial service. When she heard that Kyra was lost, they changed their plans and headed north. She contacted, Kyra's sister and brother, Ellen and Mathieu, and made plans for them to fly up to be with us. At home in Grass Valley, my brother and sister-in-law heard about Kyra, picked up my mom in the foothills of the Sierra Nevada Mountains, and made the six hour drive to the caves near the Oregon border. I was relieved they were making this effort to be with me, but it was devastating to realize the seriousness of the situation. The fact that my family would drop everything and come stand vigil for Kyra felt comforting on one level, but distressing on another.

The Rangers called a chaplain to come and visit with me.

I was exhausted and went to lie down in the RV which had now been moved away from the cave entrance and back to the Visitor Center, per orders of the Captain. Wait a minute.

Doesn't a chaplain come and speak to you when someone has died? Are they thinking the children are at the risk of dying now? I felt sick all over.

It was now 1:00 pm. The children had been lost for 18 hours. With so many cave experts using expert strategies and still not finding them, it was becoming clear how dire the situation was. The chaplain and I prayed.

I tried to focus on Kyra and Kai. I imagined them somewhere deep in the earth. Forty years after my near drowning experience, Kyra was lost in a cave. I drew from the courage I had found as an eight year old struggling to stay alive when the ocean was trying to swallow me up. That voice silently prayed to her, "DO NOT GIVE UP NOW. THIS ISNOT THE WAY YOUR LIFE IS GOING TO END."I told them to "HANG ON" and know we were searching for them. I asked them to show us where they were. I had dismissed the kidnapping theory and was seeing them lost in the cave.

Outside something new was developing. Cave enthusiasts called "spelunkers" were arriving. I could see jackets with club names like Shasta Area Grotto. Their passion for exploring caves gave new energy to this cave search where they felt most alive.

Little did I know that 75 miles away, a spelunker named Dr. Bill Broeckel, a pediatrician in Weed, was talking with his wife, Judy.

"You know, Bill, those kids have been in that cave for almost 20 hours now. I doubt they could survive another night in the cave."

"I know, but I'm on call and I've got a waiting room full of patients."

"If anyone can find those kids, you can."

At that moment, he had a hunch. He had been lost in that same cave years before when chaperoning a group of kids from his church. With a sudden determination, he got someone to take over his patients for him. Luckily he still had his cave equipment in his car from an exploration he'd been on the weekend before. He called his cave buddy, Dave, and they agreed to meet over at the Lava Beds as soon as possible.

When Dr. Bill arrived at the cave entrance later in the afternoon, the Search and Rescue operations lead officer wanted him to search in another area of the cave than where his intuition said they were. It took him awhile to convince them his "hunch" would take him to the children. At 6:00 pm, Bill and Dave headed into the cave to find the children.

They were going to an area where they would have to wriggle through on their belly through a tunnel only twelve inches high. Only panicked and terrified children trying everything they could to find a way out would have gone in there. The Rangers didn't even know about this place. It wasn't on their maps. Only spelunkers knew about it, spelunkers like

Bill and Dave who had been in this cave over seventy times since the first time Dr. Bill had been lost in it.

Only Kai and Kyra could say what truly happened next, but this is what they later told me. In the dark, damp cave they first heard muffled sounds. Each heard the other gasp in the complete darkness, with the hope of help arriving. Next they saw glaring lights from flashlights illuminating the dark and damp room they had occupied for twenty-seven hours.

"Yes!" they shouted, "We've been found!"

They heard two men's voices.

"Hello, Kyra and Kai?"

Soon the kids were devouring granola bars and fruit juice.

"Are you ready to get out of this place? There are a lot of people outside who can't wait to see you."

They gratefully nodded. Bill radioed that the children had been found.

"We're coming up!"

All of a sudden my sister, Hilary, came blasting out of the Visitor's Center and burst out screaming, "They found them! They found them!"

We all ran together in the same manner that a football team floods the field after winning a game. We screamed and hugged and jumped ecstatically. This moment felt better to me than the moment Kyra had been born.

Still, I kept a tight lid on my excitement. I wouldn't let myself believe she was really okay until I could see and hold her. It had taken a long time for the fact that they were lost to sink in, and it was going to take more time that they were found to feel tangible.

We jumped in a car and headed up to the cave entrance. It was 6:30 pm.

We saw Kai's Dad smiling widely. Kai's Mom and siblings had also arrived. People shouted that the children were all right, but I still couldn't believe it yet.

At last they walked out into the light. It was almost sunset and after being in the dark for more than a day they both squinted as their eyes adjusted to the light. I ran up and practically tackled Kyra, squeezing her tight and telling her how much I loved her. My family gathered in a big group hug. Kyra and Kai were safe again in the arms of their families.

Kyra looked up, saw my Mom and said, "Grandma, what are you doing here?" She was pale and dazed, and didn't realize that she and Kai had been in the cave for more than a day.

The Search and Rescue teams and dogs, Rangers and staff from the Visitor's Center, the spelunkers, some of the school community and local and national television reporters with cameras gathered at the cave entrance. Kyra and I walked to the waiting ambulance. The EMT's requested to examine the children before releasing them.

A huge celebration ensued. The Sheriff's auxiliary volunteers had arrived in the afternoon and had been preparing food for the team. Thankfully, a dinner of burgers, beans, and drinks intended for a search party turned into a welcome back celebration for Kyra, Kai, and the rescuers. Everyone joined this feast where we all sat at long tables and listened to Dr. Bill Broeckel tell us about his hunch. I felt a warm mood of compassion and gratitude permeates the Fire Station. Almost everyone had been closer to giving up hope than they had let on. The reprieve from agony was palpable.

It was close to 8:30 pm and my family needed some-where to stay. We found some cabins at the edge of the national park. As we drove through this wilderness area, Kyra was surprised and comforted by the fact that we were all there waiting for her. After we checked into our cabins, Kyra told us what happened.

"When Kai and I were walking out of the cave we saw some stairs. We climbed down them and into a tunnel, but when we turned around to come back, we went the wrong way. When we realized we were lost, we started running faster and faster trying to find our way out."

"We yelled for you," I said. "Didn't you hear us?"

It turns out that caves absorb sounds. They never heard us calling.

If you're stuck on a mountain, you run downhill to get off of it. In a cave, you climb up to get out. Kyra and Kai kept running down and down, deeper into the cave. The room they ended up in after shimmying through the twelve-inch tunnel was two miles deep into this cave.

When they scooted through the small tunnel and ended up in the room, they realized they should stay put in order to have a better chance of being found. They turned out their flashlights to conserve the batteries. While this was a smart idea, it was so dark in the cave that they ended up not being able to find them again. For 27 ½ hours they sat in the dark. It was fifty-five degrees and they weren't dressed for the cold. They huddled together to stay warm, a huge embarrassment for Kyra. How could she face Kai at school again?

In the cave they spoke about what was most important to them. For Kyra it was her family and Diamond, her horse. For Kai, it was his family and his friends. During these moments they wondered if they would ever be found.

As a mother of a feisty eleven year old, this was one of the most humbling and grateful experiences of my life. I learned how easily your precious child could be lost, how important it is to listen to your intuition and to engage others in believing in that intuition.

Even in your darkest hour when all hope seems lost, there are greater, unseen forces working for you, that the least likely can become your strongest allies. As a leader, always believe in the possibility of a miracle.

Chapter Three

"Intuition will tell the thinking mind where to look next."
-Jonas Salk

**Third Message:
Listen to your intuition.
Your example teaches others to do the same.**

    My grandmother, aunt and mother were my first role models for leadership. Each of them had their own nuances, as mothers who led by creating strong family relationships.
    Raised on a Tennessee tobacco farm, my grandmother, Claytie Kidder, went to college in the 1920's when not too many women did. After a few years of study, she got on a train by herself, moved to Los Angeles, found a job and place to live, and enjoyed a single life into her late twenties. Her courage and tenacity mixed with her kind and loving spirit was amazing. She adored children and once she married and had her own, she devoted herself to children by being a church preschool teacher. When I announced as a child that I wanted to be a doctor when I grew up, she always believed in me.
    My Aunt Dorothy raised a family of five children and is an intelligent and thoughtful woman and so much fun to be around. Mother and daughter relationships can be mired in conflict and when my Mom and I would get into misunderstandings; my aunt would always be a safe haven for

me. I could tell her anything and she would offer wise advice and unconditional love.

My mother, Virginia Crabb, is still going strong as she faces 90 and has always been a dedicated and loving influence in my life. At age seven she taught me about the power of intuition and this profoundly affected my life.

It was a lazy weekend afternoon. I was resting with my eyes closed, lying on my single bed up against one corner of my bedroom, with a pale pink blanket covering me. The light was off and even though there were four wood-framed windows with six panes in each one, and thin, see-through white nylon curtains covering them, sunlight only came through in the morning as this wall-faced north. The three large sycamore trees that stood sentry outside also filtered the daylight so my room had the soft, peaceful feeling of dusk even at midday.

I heard someone tiptoe quietly into my room and sit on the side of my bed. Never remembering this happening be-fore, I lay silently enjoying this mysterious attention. I wondered if whoever was there was going to tickle me awake. I held my lips tightly together to keep from smiling. I was even more surprised when this person, an angel, really, started softly stroking my forehead as an introduction to one of the most astonishing moments of my life.

This must have been what it felt like in my mother's womb, where all my needs were continually met. I melted into a puddle of bliss from this sweet, quiet attention. No words were spoken. If I could have asked for a moment like this with my mom before, knowing how completely adored I felt, I would have asked in a heartbeat. Being so out of the ordinary made this moment that more special, and I didn't want it to end. You see, I was born in the 1950's and our family didn't show much physical affection except an infrequent goodnight peck on the cheek before bed.

After she stroked my forehead, she ran her fingers gently through the top of my brown, curly hair and massaged my scalp with just the right touch. I had no idea how sacred the touch from another human could feel, especially from my mother. My whole body felt warm on the inside and the outside. This filled me up in ways I didn't know existed.

Mothers are so wise and mine was setting the stage to tell me something, to imprint a profound teaching in my soul. The lights were low, and she started to speak.

"I want to tell you the story of your birth."

This was my seventh year and I opened my big brown eyes wide and sat up a little. She positioned my pillow under my back.

"Does that feel good?"

"Yes, Mom. Tell me what happened when I was born!"

"You were three weeks overdue when I went into labor."

She slid off the corner of the bed, sat on the hardwood floor, which was the color of toasted walnuts, and looked into my eyes. I'm sure my eyes were as big as they could stretch.

"I was having a difficult time delivering you. There was my doctor and two obstetrical technicians in the delivery room pushing on my tummy trying to help get you out. Turns out, you were in the breech position."

"Breech? What is that?"

"That is when you come out bottom first instead of head first."

"Eeww."

The corners of my mouth turned down.

"Dr. Alward, my doctor, said even being in a breech position, the baby usually just pops out."

"Oh."

"With all that pushing, you finally came out. I was thrilled you were a girl! After each of your brothers, I'd been trying for a girl and finally, I had you!"

Her smile was wide as a waxing moon. She was so beautiful. Every cell of my being was smiling, too.

"You were big, too, what with being almost a month overdue; 9 pounds, 3 ounces. No wonder I couldn't deliver you very easily!"

"We brought you home and everything was going pretty well, that is as well as could be expected for having three boys and now a new infant. Dougie was only 18 months older than you so I was very tired running after him and nursing you."

"Hmmm."

I hung on to her every word. We'd never shared a moment like this before, just the two of us. The whole house was quiet, which was rare in a houseful of boys.

"When you were about a month old, your dad and I celebrated our 12th wedding anniversary. I had arranged several anniversary cards on the mantle over the fireplace so I could enjoy seeing them. One day I noticed a card had fallen down and when I bent down to pick it up; all of a sudden I started hemorrhaging. I fainted to the floor."

I didn't know what that meant, but it didn't sound good. Not wanting her to stop talking, I didn't ask any questions.

"Luckily, your grandmother, my mother, was there. She would come over every morning and help out with you and your brothers. She helped me get up and into my bed. There was a big pool of blood on the floor."

I couldn't stop my hand from flying up to cover my mouth. Now I knew what hemorrhaging meant. I held my breath.

"I remember it was a Saturday morning. Your father had taken our car to do the shopping for the week. Mother called Dr. Alward and he said to get to the hospital right away. We waited for your dad to get back and as soon as he did, they put the seat down in the back of the station wagon, laid me down, and set out for the emergency room. Your Dad drove fast and even ran a red light. A policeman saw him speeding and pulled us over. He told the officer the situation and the officer escorted us to the hospital. Your Grandma stayed with you kids."

I was glad we weren't alone when Mom had to go to the hospital, but I just wanted to hear about the rest of the story.

"What happened next?" I eagerly said.

"We got to the emergency room and Dr. Alward examined me. By this point I was in shock because I had lost so much blood, and I was shivering and shaking. He gave me transfusions to replace the blood I was losing and said he wanted to take me into surgery and do a curettement to stop the bleeding.

"I didn't know what that meant either, but it didn't sound very good.

"I don't know how to describe what happened next, but I call it intuition coming to my rescue. It was this feeling I had that told me not to go through with the operation. I didn't feel good, but I just wanted to rest and see how I felt in the morning.'"

"The doctor said, 'Mrs. Crabb, it's important that we do this surgery tonight and not wait until the morning,' but I told him 'No, I just need to rest tonight and see about it in the morning.'"

"'Uh-huh' was all he said."

"Dr. Alward was a good doctor. He had delivered you kids, except for Terry, all of your cousins, and even Uncle Ron. He worked at the Good Samaritan Hospital, one of the finest hospitals in Los Angeles where you were born and where I was a patient.

"After Dr. Alward left my bedside, he consulted with another doctor, a Dr. Henrickson, a gynecologist, which means he specialized in the treatments of female organs, and they decided to do a different kind of surgery in the morning. It was called an exploratory surgery where they made an incision in my belly, went inside, and looked around to see why I was bleeding.

"Yuck!"

"I know. They took me into the operating room early the next morning."

"Oh."

"After the surgery when I was back in my hospital room, both Dr. Alward and Dr. Hendrickson came to speak with me."

My eyebrows went up and my forehead crinkled.

"Mrs. Crabb, we want you to know you just saved your own life.

"Really?" Mom said.

"Your uterus had erupted into small pieces all over the inside of your abdomen. This is very rare. You were bleeding internally from an artery that had a clot attached to it. If I had gone in last night to do the curettement, I would have dislodged the clot and you would have bled to death. Since you wouldn't allow that, I planned the exploratory procedure with Dr. Henrickson and we were able to find the problem and correct it."

I took a deep breath and Mom paused. I felt tingly all over. There was a hushed silence. Mom took a deep breath, too and then continued talking.

"I was still very weak. The next night I felt like I was in a dream where I could see this bright light at the end of a tunnel.

But there was a voice that said, *'Here's a rope. Just reach up and grab onto it.*

"There was another long pause where I couldn't tell if Mom was going to cry as it looked as if she might. She was so strong.

"Our family was active in the American Legion, since your Dad had been in the Air Force. A lot of the men donated blood for me as I needed more transfusions."

"Oh."

My face felt hot and tears filled my eyes. I wondered why my mom had to go through this. I leaned into her and let out a deep breath with such a relief. Hearing how close I came to growing up without a mom was truly a revelation.

"I got to go back home about eight days later. I couldn't wait to get back to see you. Before all this happened, I had been nursing you, but Grandma had to start feeding you formula in a bottle. I was still pretty weak and had gotten down to under a hundred pounds. Mother took such good care of me. I could not have survived without her. She stayed with us during the day, taking care of you kids while nursing me back to health, and then would go back to her home at night to be with Uncle Ron."

"Uh-huh."

"So, Mary Beth, what I want you to remember is to always, **ALWAYS** listen to your intuition. You just never know when it will save your life."

I could tell this was an important lesson, but I didn't know at age seven what intuition was or how to use it. Maybe it was something I would know when I got older.

Thankfully I did learn to understand and use my intuition. It is as simple as sensing when your child is lying to you, or recognizing when something is just "off" in your life.

Recently, as I was asking my mother about this experience, she asked if my intuition had ever given me a nudge so if I told her about this experience.

Prior to being involved in a few car accidents, I have often felt a strong tug on the back of my shoulders. It is like someone is grabbing me by the shoulders and jolting my awareness to notice something. The last time this happened, it was close to my 55th birthday. I was reaching into my mailbox when I felt that tug. I looked up to the sky, nodded my head, and said silently to myself, "I'll be careful."

Two weeks later I was going to dinner to celebrate my birthday with my daughter and some friends. We were stopped at the traffic lights close to our home. The light turned green, but my foot didn't automatically press down on the accelerator. I was frozen for a moment in time. Just then, a large SUV raced through the intersection of the four lane highway, running a red light. If I had moved the car the moment the light turned green, I would have been broadsided and probably killed. Later I had an "aha" moment about the tug on my shoulders a few weeks before warning me to heighten my awareness.

As I look back on my life, when has my intuition not spoken to me? The words "Listen to your intuition" were in-grained in my soul when I was seven years old. When I was caught in the rip tide and being rolled around in a soupy sea of sand and salt water and almost drowned, when I couldn't see or feel which way was "up" to catch a breath of air, my intuition must have guided me. When my daughter, Kyra, was lost and the search team wasn't sure if they had come out of the cave or had been kidnapped, I sensed they were deep in the cave and sent a message from my spirit to theirs, telling them to hold on, that help was coming. When my older daughter, Ellen, was staring into space in a period of dissociating behavior, I knew I had to find her the best psychiatric care available and was led to the Langley Porter Institute after my intuition told me who to call.

I believe your intuition is always available for you—an inner compass if you want it—leading you to the right actions for your life. It is always available for you to access by just closing your eyes and asking, "Is this decision right for me?" Listen until you hear or feel an answer and then take action on what you hear. You might already know how well using your intuition can work in your life, but if this is a new concept, close your eyes and be still for 15 minutes; listen for some direction. The more you do this, the easier the answers will come.

As a leader bringing a vision into reality, you will need to make decisions every step of the process. Some decisions will take you close to producing the result you want, some won't. Trust your intuition to bring you the best decision in every moment.

Part Two

~

Find the Gifts in Challenges

Chapter Four

"If facts are the seeds that later produce knowledge and wisdom, then the emotions and the impressions of the senses are the fertile soil in which the seeds must grow."
–Rachel Carson

**Message Four:
Feel your feelings from the challenges you face.
This will open your heart and expand your capacity for compassion, courage, and extraordinary leadership.**

When you or someone close to you is diagnosed with a serious illness, every part of your life calls for leadership. To navigate successfully requires being in sync with your mind, body, and soul. This experience deepens you in every way, if you let it.

"See these large white and dark areas on the pictures I just took during your colonoscopy?"

The gastroenterologist had taken Bob, my husband, and myself aside in a corridor of our local hospital and showed us the pictures.

"These look like advanced tumors. We took a biopsy and will have confirmation in a week, but I'm referring you to an oncologist."

Bob's skin turned pale and his face had that stoic look like an animal faking death to avoid being attacked by predator.

I'm sure I stopped breathing until the doctor closed the picture in the file then walked away.

On May 28, 1998, Bob was diagnosed with Stage IV colon cancer. The graphic photos from his colonoscopy showing the deadly invasive tumors left me with a feeling of dread and no sense of possibility for a cure. The oncologist said that although many cancer treatments had evolved over the years and improved patients' chances for a cure or living longer, there hadn't been any new treatments discovered for colon cancer. This journey we were to go on would test us in ways we couldn't imagine, especially our capacity to experience a wide range of profound emotions.

Bob received chemotherapy concurrently with radiation and I witnessed his tall, strong, lean Swedish runner's body become weak and ravaged. The side effect that was most debilitating for him was the uncontrollable diarrhea, which lasted even after the treatments stopped. They said his double whammy therapy would either give him six months or a few years to live. He was only 54 years old, in the prime of his life, and had worked very hard on building his civil engineering business. We had three kids in college, one in high school, and a five-year old daughter at home.

Bob went on to have a fairly decent life after his six months of treatment. Then one morning in late May of 1999, he awakened with severe abdominal pain and vomiting. The doctors said to go to the hospital where he was diagnosed with a bowel obstruction.

We decided to go to the Sacramento doctor who had done the surgery of removing the colon tumors, over an hour's drive from home. The MRI's showed the cancer had spread to the liver. His colon had twisted on itself as a result of adhesions or scarring from the first surgery. The surgeon took him into surgery and released the obstruction. He and the oncologist didn't have any treatment to offer him for the apparent liver metastases except to suggest getting a new type of scan called a PET scan. More difficult news en-sued; the cancer had now spread to the sinuses in his head. The doctors again gave him six months to live.

It is amazing how in the grand plan of life, Bob had married me, a former oncology nurse. In nursing school they taught us to "be professional" and "don't let your feelings show to your patients."

When I started working with cancer patients in the late 1970's as a young nurse, I was surprised to see this cardinal rule didn't hold sway in real life nursing. If the patients I cared for were having horrible side effects from the chemo or radiation, or were experiencing the end of their life be-cause the treatment was no longer working, the team of nurses felt and showed our feelings. It felt so good to be "real" with our patients and their families because it was difficult to deal with all that human suffering, no matter if you were in the bed with them or watching from their bedside. There was a whole lot of hugging and tears shed on that Oncology floor.

I remembered that when the oncologists ran out of protocols to give our patients, they referred them to MD Ander-son Cancer Institute, the world-renowned teaching hospital of the University of Texas in Houston. I suggested to Bob that we go see what new treatments they could offer him.

Our civil engineering business was thriving, and Bob was the principal engineer in the firm. It was summer and our now 6-year-old daughter, Kyra, was out of school and needed lots of attention. I wondered, "How were we going to manage a trip to Texas?"

Wise and *Ready* to Rise

Bob was tall, handsome and lanky, and his spirit and energy inspired all who knew him. A gentle giant who didn't like violence, he was very manly with well-defined muscular arms and big hands chiseled from the years of construction he had done. With a big heart and vision, he had spent years working to end world hunger and create a more sustainable life on earth that protected the environment. He loved engaging in personal growth and development and taught follow-up seminars to graduates of the Landmark Education weekend program called The Forum.

A creator, Bob had built several homes, businesses, and pieces of furniture. His first home was a Frank Lloyd Wright inspired round house where all the rooms had curved walls. Always busy doing something, he worked late into the night and got up early in the morning. His life was worth all the energy and resources needed to go Texas, to him, our family, and those who knew him.

Actually, the more that cancer kept invading his life, the softer and more spiritual Bob became. He asked everyone around him to not use violent terms in association with cancer. "Fighting, struggle, or invading" was replaced with "dancing and cooperating" with what cancer was bringing to his life. One of the greatest gifts of having cancer, we dis-covered, was that you have a sense that your days of living are more finite and it becomes more important to savor each one. That, he did. He inspired everyone around him to do the same.

Bob wanted to see how MD Anderson could help. I did some research to see if there was any treatment for the liver or sinus metastases. There was little information available except for a few paragraphs about experimental ablation surgeries for the liver metastases and Gamma radiation knife treatments for the sinus metastases. I called and started the long procedure of getting an appointment.

It took several weeks, but in mid-July, 1999, we figured out a way to keep the business functioning, arranged child-care for Kyra, and flew off to Houston.

Mid-July is about the worst time to be in Texas. It is so hot and muggy. We stayed at a budget hotel because we had no idea how long we would be there. The room was well worn from all the guests who had probably come on a similar journey as we had, seeing if MD Anderson could help them treat, and hopefully cure, their cancer.

The next morning we went to the center, carrying Bob's medical information including x-rays and scans from his en-tire "dance" thus far with cancer. When we walked into this gigantic building, we saw a maze of different colored lines painted on the floor, each one leading to a department that focuses on a different part of the body. We followed the green line to Bob's appointment in the Gastroenterology Department, and we met with a team of doctors, residents, and interns who daily saw patients with rare presentations of cancer. The spreading of colon cancer to the sinus was extremely rare.

We didn't spend much time in the examining room. The main doctor had a Russian name and accent. He quickly examined Bob, looked at his scans, and referred him to the Head and Neck so they could focus on the sinus metastasis. When we got the appointment slip from the medical secretary we noticed it was scheduled for another week.

I looked at her and whined, "But we're from California. Is there any way we could have an appointment sooner?"

She looked at me like I was crazy. Earlier in the waiting room I had seen patients who looked as if they had traveled from many different countries. At least we actually lived in the United States.

"Sorry, this is the earliest appointment we have."

I quickly understood and resolved myself to the wait. I thought of all the other cancer patients staying at the low budget hotels that surrounded the cancer center, each one waiting their turn for their next appointment. Shoulders slumped; we got into our rented sedan and drove back to the hotel.

After a day or so making the best of the wait by going to tourist areas like the beach town of Galveston and the visiting the NASA space center, we were thoroughly bored. Not ones to watch much TV and having read as much as we cared to, I found a business center with computers available nearby. As this was before smart phones, I got an email account and started sending updates to our families and friends to while away some of the time and keep connected with our community back home.

Eventually, I came up with an idea to bring some fun into this experience. Neither one of us had ever been to New Orleans. We were paying for a hotel as it was and we had a rental car. Since summer is the hottest and least desirable time to visit "The Big Easy", hotel rates were at rock bottom. I got us a lovely suite for just about the same price as we were paying for our discount room in Houston. We loaded up our suitcases and took off on an adventure.

The highway from Texas to New Orleans was elevated and we could look down on the braided streams and water-filled swamps. I imagined lots of alligators, crawfish, and catfish swimming in those areas. To me, Bob's cancer felt like an alligator; it was waiting quietly, being fed by something invisible, and when we least expected, it would jump out and bite us.

It was Bob's cancer, but when your husband receives this diagnosis it affects you and your family as well. Just like when I became pregnant with Kyra six years before and we happily announced, "We're pregnant!" to everyone; as the cancer progressed I felt that this cancer was just as big a part of my life as my pregnancy was to Bob's. He had to experience the physical effects of the disease and treatment; the rest of our family and I had to deal with the fallout.

As we drove into New Orleans, we agreed it had the feel of a southern San Francisco. The architecture was stately and historic. We easily found our hotel and settled in.

Brimming with curiosity, we got dressed to go out on the town. After walking just a few blocks to the French Quarter and even though it was night time, we became drenched in sweat due to the humidity and heat. We dined on an outside upstairs porch that was decorated with ornate rod iron railing typical of the New Orleans style. We ate the most succulent gulf shrimp. I had never tasted any so good. Creole spices wafted throughout the restaurant. The distraction of being in a city that was so alive and away from the depressing waiting game in Houston was beginning to work. New Orleans is one never-ending party with jazz music coming from almost every street corner bar, and tourists tipsy from their "blue hurricane" drinks they grasped in their hands as they strolled down Bourbon Street. This atmosphere buoyed our spirits.

Even with the frivolity of New Orleans, being a tourist becomes old after a while. We headed back to Houston after four days and hoped to avoid a hurricane that was roaring into the Gulf area. It felt as if it was one catastrophe after an-other! We were so relieved when the storm was downgraded to a tropical storm and ended up hitting land away from the Houston area. The well-worn budget hotel took us back, yet now we yearned for the beautiful suite we had left back in New Orleans.

The alarm awoke us early the next morning so we could make Bob's 9:00 am appointment at the Head and Neck Clinic. A handsome doctor with slicked back dark hair and twinkling blue eyes welcomed us as we entered the room. Although he said this metastasis was rare, he felt confident he could de-bulk the tumor and refer Bob for Gamma Knife radiation back home in California. His confidence felt like a safety net that was saving us from the alligator. We asked how quickly he could schedule the surgery due to our having waited a week to see him. The surgeon made Bob a priority and within a few days, he had his surgery.

Those two hours he was in surgery were some of the loneliest of my life. Whenever Bob had been in surgery back in California, there had always been family or friends with me. I had never felt so alone, so far from support and shoulders to lean on. Thankfully the moment came when I was called into the recovery room where Bob was waking up and was soon assisted into a wheelchair. I was given instructions to pick up antibiotics and pain medications at the pharmacy on our way out.

Bob was still groggy and had packing in his nose and gauze dressing like a sling under his nostrils. I wheeled him along one of the painted lines on the floor that said "Pharmacy." Eventually I made it through the maze of twists and turns along scuffed grey linoleum to a beautiful several stories high-ceilinged waiting area. There were long lines queuing up in front of a bank of windows with a few pharmacy techs behind the glass, scooping up the prescriptions patients slipped from the stainless steel trough outside the window counters far in the distance. There were at least fifty people in front of us waiting in line.

My body stiffened as the thought, *"This doesn't seem right"*, circled in my head. The conversation in my mind was saying, *"Here's Bob, sitting in a wheelchair, after just having tumors removed from his head, and we have to wait in line for who knows how long to get his medicine?"* My fingers wrapped tighter around the wheelchair handles. My jaw tightened.

After waiting for fifteen minutes and not moving much, Bob started squirming in the wheelchair. I wished I had the pain pills NOW so I could give him one. *"This just isn't right to make a surgery patient wait in line forever for his meds."* My breathing became faster and shallower. *"Why don't they have more techs helping people? There are three vacant windows and the lines keep getting longer!"*

All of a sudden blood started dripping down Bob's face from his nose. Without waiting another second, I pushed Bob's wheelchair up to the vacant window and knocked on it. When no one noticed me or came up to help, my anxiety and frustration turned into tears. Not one to cry much, and not wanting to be vulnerable in front of a large group of strangers, I couldn't hold the tears in. It felt as if I was the vessel for all the tears for everyone in this MD Anderson Cancer Center to flow through. It felt as if I was shedding tears for all of the devastating news people were receiving; tears for the days of waiting for the next appointment; tears for needing more help and no one available to provide the needed assistance.

Suddenly a man behind the glass saw my tears and ran over to help. He asked what I needed through the microphone behind the glass with a panicked look on his face and breathlessness to his voice.

"My husband just had surgery and he's bleeding," I said as my lower lip quivered and I gulped down a sob.

I could feel everyone's eyes on me in that waiting area. I had somehow managed to open gauze dressing from the bag they gave me in the recovery room and swab up the blood and put pressure where it was coming from.

"I need his antibiotics...*sniff*...and pain pills...sob... so I can take him back to hotel...*cough*. He needs to lie down!" "Okay, okay", the pharmacist, said. "Slide the prescription under the window and I'll get them for you as quickly as I can."

I grabbed gauze square as the first one was al-most saturated and it wasn't stopping the bleeding. I could tell I didn't have enough gauze in the bag to staunch the stream of blood. I also didn't have enough tears for all of the sorrow in that waiting room either.

I watched as he dashed back behind the high metal shelves that were stocked with boxes of pharmaceuticals. He ran back up to another staff member who put the meds in a bottle, labeled them and dropped them into a white paper pharmacy bag, ran back over to me, and slid them under the glass. It felt like only one bottle was in the bag.

"There you go, ma'am."

I opened up the white paper bag and only found one bottle of pain pills.

"Sir?"

The pharmacist had walked away.

"Sir!" I said louder as I knocked on the window.

He ran back again but was less attentive, not wanting to deal with my red, tear stained face again, and the face of sorrow and frustration everyone in the waiting area was attempting to hide.

"Ma'am?"

"There are only the pain pills here. Where are the antibiotics? They told me you had the order for them and for me to pick them up at the pharmacy."

"Let me check on this, ma'am."

"Please hurry! My husband is bleeding! He needs to lie down, now!"

"Yes, ma'am!"

I saw the back of his light brown haired head as he ran to a phone and made a call. His conversation went on for so long. I kept pressure on Bob's nose with that last piece of gauze.

"Sir! "

I banged on the window again. He didn't turn his head toward me. I needed more gauze. Bob looked very pale and uncomfortable. The pharmacist finally slammed the phone down and handed a paper to the staff person who went to typing on the computer.

"Sir!" I banged again.

"Yes, ma'am. I have the order and we're filling it as fast as we can."

"Thank you, and could you please give me some gauze? I'm running out and my husband is bleeding from his surgery."

The pharmacist's face turned greenish and his lips crinkled. He sort of shrugged his shoulders helplessly. You'd think I'd asked him for the moon, even in this huge hospital. *Doesn't anyone have some gauze?*

Again he leapt into action and ran behind the large beige steel shelves. I saw him come back into my line of vision as he stopped by a fellow staff member, grabbed another white bag, and ran back over to our window, stuffing the bag through the stainless trough.

"Here you go, ma'am, and I'm so sorry for your wait. There's some gauze there, too."

There was a collective sigh in that waiting room. Bob's body started to relax as I put the bag in his lap and started wheeling him away. I felt every eye on me, but I knew I had handled that difficult situation with as much diplomacy as I could, and my tears were an authentic expression of my exasperation of the situation.

I don't think I took another deep breath until an hour later when we were back in our budget hotel room, the bleeding had stopped, and Bob had drifted off to sleep. I was exhausted from this long, emotional day. *"Better keep breathing and resting while you can. There is another "dance" with this cancer waiting back in California for you"* my inner voice said to me.

I learned from this experience that an effective leader is in touch with their feelings and acts with emotional intelligence. This leader who is present with their emotions and expresses them authentically can evoke trust from the team. According to the website, Mind Tools, emotional intelligence (EI) is "the ability to understand and manage both your own emotions and those of the people around you. Persons with a high degree of emotional intelligence usually know what they're feeling, what it means, and how their emotions can affect other people." For leaders, having emotional intelligence is essential for creating the results you are intending.

When emotional experiences come into your life, how do you process them? Many of us are taught as children not to feel them. Phrases such as, *"Don't cry like a baby. Stop crying* or *I'll give you something to cry about! That's enough, now."* have influenced our upbringing. Well-meaning or frustrated parents do their best to prepare their children for life's challenges. But, when we meet one of life's defining moments, it can be those very feelings that rise and need to be expressed for us to be able to find meaning in what seems so unbearable.

Feel your feelings. Discover what they mean to you. Communicate them in a way that has meaning for others. This builds trust in your team from which you can create the results you have intended.

Chapter Five

*"Be a Columbus to whole new continents
and worlds within you,
opening new channels, not of trade, but of thought."*
–Henry David Thoreau

**Message Five:
Open up to all the good that wants to come your way and your vision becomes realized.**

When faced with an ongoing challenge, there are a few ways you can approach it. One is "it's a tragedy" and "it's only going to get worse"; the other is that "every moment you will attract all that you need to keep moving forward on your journey through life". This story shows how so much good came to me even as Bob's cancer progressed.

Bob went through surgery on his liver and radiation to his sinus metastases then had a year of freedom to live his life. He traveled to Ecuador and had healings with indigenous shamans. We joined a spiritual community that sup-ported us with so much caring, and ongoing healings. We truly felt loved and supported by our family and community
.But the cancer and problems in our relationship became so great that I felt a deep calling to separate from Bob. I didn't want a divorce because I loved him at a deep, soul level.

Perhaps subconsciously I was preparing for when he wouldn't be here on earth with me. My body felt exhausted in a way I had never known because of all of the physical and emotional support I had directed Bob's way during his ill-ness. I listened to this call for rest and individuation and decided to take some time to heal myself. Sensing Bob had some unfinished personal matters he wanted to pursue; I wanted him to feel free to live his life fully, unencumbered by any judgments or conditions from me. I hoped we could each grow in ways that would bring us back together to create a deeper love and relationship. By separating, I hoped more good would come our way, but I didn't know what that would be just yet.

I listened to my intuition on this step, yet also feared judgment from my peers and family. How could she leave her husband who still could die from cancer anytime? That seems so selfish. These thoughts swirled in my head, but that deeper calling for health and wholeness won out and I moved across town. Bob and I still shared a deep connection, even with the separation, especially through our shared custody of Kyra.

About a year later, the cancer returned. There was no further treatment available for him. This time it was the sinus tumor that was growing fast and starting to press on his brain, especially on his speech center. He was still man-aging our engineering business, but over a period of just a week, he stopped being able to speak his thoughts. Al-though still coherent, he had to use hand gestures and write things down to communicate. A local engineering firm, Holdrege and Kull, graciously helped us keep running our business as Bob's health started to fail. Time and again when Bob was no longer able to do the things that needed to be done, the community stepped up to fill in the gaps.

When I was picking up Kyra from Bob's one day, I noticed a plastic bucket on the deck of his rented home. It had melted and burned into the deck because he had unconsciously put hot coals and ashes from the wood stove in the bucket. I knew right then it was no longer safe for him to live alone. I also knew in my heart and soul that I would come back to take care of him in his final days, and those days were now here.

Bob and I met with the Hospice team, and even with these new symptoms, he was reluctant to accept what was happening. I told him I was moving back in to be with him, that he would not be alone. He smiled and tears welled up in his eyes. There was a moment when that deep love we'd always had for each other came present. No words were needed. I could sense this would be a time for us to heal the past and have a loving final chapter of our relationship.

We called the family to let them know about his prognosis. To be referred to Hospice, one has to have a terminal diagnosis and a life expectancy of six months or less. It was mid-October, 2001, and I doubted if he would make it to the New Year.

Bob was so amazing during those final weeks and most of the time he had a smile on his face. His birthday was the day before Halloween. We threw him a combined birthday and retirement party, as he wanted the kind of celebration that Morrie had in the book *"Tuesdays With Morrie,"* where he was present at his own memorial service before he died so that he could experience all the love and appreciation people wanted to show him. We sent out invitations to friends, family, colleagues, and our community, asking them to bring a poem, story, song, or some memory to share with Bob. It was his living memorial where he got to take in how much he was loved and how in his life he had made such a difference. He reveled in it.

I brought a wheelchair in the car in case he needed it, and by the end of the evening we had to use it to get him to the car. He actually asked to leave his own party; he was in so much pain. I silently had wished and prayed for some miraculous recovery, but this was a sign that my hope for a cure just wasn't going to happen. I ordered a hospital bed the next day.

His pain and weakness were showing all of us that Bob was getting closer to the end of his life. The children showed they wanted to be a part of this experience by coming home. None of us had any idea it would go the way it did.

Mathieu, Bob's twenty-year old son, was in his second year of college. His mother, Hilary, was very concerned about how his dad's dying would affect him. She was the first to step up in such a magnanimous way to help.

"Have you thought about Thanksgiving?" she asked me. My husband was dying from cancer. Normally one to make a big fuss over the holidays and cook and entertain family and friends, I knew I wouldn't have the time or energy to do so this year.

"You know, with everything going on with Bob, I really haven't thought about it."

"Well good, because I have. Walter and I would like to come over and cook Thanksgiving dinner for you and your family."

Hilary and Walter had just gotten engaged and she wanted to come make her ex-husband, his wife and their family a holiday meal? I was floored! I didn't even have to ask; the support was just coming our way.

"Do you have enough place settings for everyone? I can pack up my china and crystal and make this a holiday to remember."

"I haven't even thought about who would come, and all my nice dishes are packed away at my house. Let me ask Bob about whom he'd like to have at Thanksgiving and I'll get back to you."

The house Bob had rented when we separated didn't have a large dining area. We'd have to bring in some folding tables and chairs. He said he just wanted close family there. We invited the adult kids, so with Walter and Hilary that meant nine of us were going to be present for the dinner. After the meal, we went out to the big pond on the property. The kids loved going out there, fishing or skipping rocks. It was a place they could blow off steam and make sense of this time when they were slowly saying goodbye to their dad. It was as if nature opened its arms wide to safely hold them.

Bob's oldest son, Chris, lived in the area. Jenny, his eldest daughter and her husband Damon, lived three hours away in the East San Francisco Bay area. Ellen, my oldest daughter and Bob's stepdaughter, lived in Sacramento. Mathieu was attending UCLA and lived in Los Angeles. We turned the huge second bedroom into a "dormitory" with four beds. Along with the couch, all the kids had a place to sleep. We set up Bob's hospital bed in the study off of the living room. Our bed was out in the sunroom alcove that had windows all around. We loved looking out at the birds and wildlife and that beautiful pond in the distance. He stayed in the hospital bed during the day, but still crawled in next to me at night. Every day he got a little weaker, eating less and sleeping more.

Hospice came regularly to check on him. Dr. Brad Miller, the Medical Director, even made a home visit. He talked to Bob about his doubts of a life after death and gave him some videos to watch. After that week, I saw that Bob seemed to be more at peace. The creases in his face looked softer.

Jenny stayed after Thanksgiving, as she just wanted to be close to her father. We set up the other bedroom for her. The next weekend her mom, Lynn, Bob's first wife, came from her home and business in Mendocino to stay. She brought food, friendship, and a caring presence especially for Chris and Jenny, but extended her graciousness to Kyra, Ellen, and me. Lynne would cook and clean to help me out as Bob was starting to need more care.

Ellen would go back and forth to Sacramento, staying as long as her emotions could take watching Bob's process, then going back home to regroup.

Our community constantly asked how they could help. With the house bulging with family, we needed food to feed everybody. A friend took on organizing meals and almost every night we had a hot dish to enjoy, often with leftovers for lunch the next day.

One of Bob's best friend's, Michael, didn't just want to send a meal. He and his wife, Saskia, came over every Tues-day night and made us a wonderful meal. They didn't just bring food, but added a real sense of joy and flair to the evenings. One night in their determination to celebrate Bob's life and their friendship every time they came over, they made us all laugh with a silly "toe painting" session. They brought a rainbow selection of nail polish and painted every one of Bob's toes a different color. We all laughed so hard and it took a lot of the drudgery and loneliness out of this dying process.

By mid-December, Bob got weaker and he stayed in the hospital bed all the time. Mathieu left school to come be with his dad, as we just didn't know how much longer he would live. Hilary took time off from work, too, and came when Lynn went back home to her husband and business. She would cook, clean, play with Kyra, giving loving attention to all of the children and even help me with Bob when I needed it.

Damon came up on the weekends and brought food and helped cook, bring in wood, and kept the two woodstoves burning. This was an older farmhouse and only had wood heat. Always a tremendous support to his wife, Jenny, he lent his broad shoulders to this family effort.

Ellen and the kids wanted to give Bob a really great Christmas so they decorated a tree and filled the floor underneath it with gifts. I wasn't in the mood to celebrate, but didn't discourage their expression. Mathieu and Hilary are Jewish, so he and Kyra made latke's, lit the Menorah, and played dreidel games too. We had a multi-family, multi-religious holiday and end-of-life experience going on and were truly opening to all the good that life offered us.

At night we would sit around the fire in the living room and be together with Bob just off to the right in his hospital bed. There were chairs around his bed so people could sit with him while he was awake. The girls were knitting scarves and things for Christmas presents, or just to have a way to focus their thoughts on something other than Bob dying. There was joy and laughter along with the undercurrent of sorrow. The acceptance of our extended family all coming together in such a selfless and welcoming way was comforting to all of us. There was always more than one mother there to hold that space of compassion and love.

At one point when Lynn was visiting, Hilary hopped into my bed that night due to lack of enough sleeping arrangements, and that was the moment of her becoming a true sister to me. It didn't seem odd at all. Having never grown up with a sister, I sensed a long wished dream of having one coming true. She was an expert of managing logistics for food, cleaning, laundry, and most importantly, the emotional status of the kids. I leaned on all she offered from her kind and generous heart.

Bob's pain and nursing needs became an around-the-clock concern. After bathing him, turning him every two hours, giving him pain meds, and being his primary care giver all day and night, I was becoming exhausted and sleep deprived. I hired some nurses to sit with him at night so I would have the energy to take care of him the rest of the time.

The days wore on for all of us.

Bob slipped into a coma, but even though he didn't wake up, he was moaning loudly, hour after hour. I gave him the ordered sedation medications and strong pain relievers, but the moaning continued. Kyra was now out of school for Christmas vacation, so we arranged play dates with friends to keep her away from this excruciating situation. It was hard on everyone.

Finally, one morning about 5:00 am, I couldn't take it anymore and called the on call Hospice nurse. An RN my-self who had years of helping patients die, I couldn't make Bob comfortable and I felt helpless.

"He's moaning so loudly all the time. I've given all the medications he can have and nothing seems to help," I told the nurse."

I hear you. It must be really wearing on your nerves."

"Yes, it is. No one can sleep and then I still have to carefor him all day. I'm exhausted.

"You know, Bob's a really tough guy."

"Yes, he's always been that way, not a complainer, so that is why this is even harder to listen to."

"Maybe the reason he is moaning is not due to pain; maybe he's moaning as a way to let his life go."

I paused and let that in. A light went on inside me.

"Oh my gosh…I think you are right. This makes total sense to me."

This change in perspective made it easier for me to listen to Bob's moaning. He didn't show other signs of pain like furrowing his brow or having shortness of breath; he was just letting his big, strong life force out through his voice so that he could transition to the next stage for his spirit.

As with many people who are dying, there can be a moment when they awaken from a coma and reconnect with loved ones. This happened for Bob one evening when I had gone out to our company Christmas party at a local restaurant. With so much upheaval in our business with Bob's dying, I felt I needed to be present at this event. When I left, Bob was lying on his side and was unresponsive, which meant he was no longer opening his eyes, talking, eating, or drinking. Even though the family was with him, I had hired a nurse to take care of his physical needs.

When I returned, he was sitting up in bed, wide awake, with a big smile on his face, watching a football game on TV and talking about it with the family. He was acting like he had just woken up from a little nap, but in reality he had been unresponsive for several days. I was in shock, but de-lighted for another chance to be with him. I walked over to his bed and kissed him on the cheek. He was more interested in the football game than seeing me. Go figure!

As the days of watching Bob lingering in this state of dying, I felt weariness come over me. It was the same feeling I'd had when I had separated from Bob a year before. I felt a strong urge to take a self-care break. At this point I'd been being a caregiver for Bob and the family for a month without a break. I decided to hire around-the-clock nurses and go back to my house for a few days. This was such a difficult thing for me to do. Even though I only lived ten minutes away, I knew there was a chance Bob could die when I was gone for the 3-day break I gave myself. Could I live with that decision if this happened? My inner compass let me know that if I didn't take a break, I would get sick. I prayed that Bob would still be there when I returned.

I took boxes of pictures and spent some time placing favorites of Bob and me into a collage as a Christmas gift to him, if he was still with us then. This turned out to be away I could grieve the eminent passing of my dear Bob. A friend offered to give me a massage, which I gratefully accepted. I took time to rest and get good sleep at night. I am such a sensitive person that I need quiet time to recharge my batteries. By the end of those three days, I was ready to return to assisting Bob and the family.

I was surprised to see how much Bob had failed in those three days. He was so much thinner and wasn't waking up again. If I wasn't providing his nursing care, doing laundry, or other chores, I was sitting vigil at his bedside. Often one of the kids would join me. His breathing was getting weaker and weaker.

Christmas morning was one of the most difficult times for me. He looked so pale and his breathing was now irregular. It seemed to me at any moment we would witness his last breath. All of us gathered around his bed. Ellen made little messages on white pieces of paper cut in the shapes of hearts and stars that said peace, love, acceptance, healing and joy, and placed them on top of his blankets. We all had different opinions about religion and spirituality in our family, but I don't think anyone there would disagree when I said it was a sacred moment. A sudden wave of sadness came over me. If I could have scooped Bob up and held him in my arms right then, I would have. Instead, I just gave him little love hugs on his arms, legs and torso as my eyes filled with tears.

I couldn't believe it would be Christmas Day that he would finally die and secretly wished it would happen on any other day than this one. Kyra was eight years old and chomping at the bit to open presents and her stocking. All of the stockings we had filled the night before lay bulging and unopened around the fireplace, and the presents were still wrapped and overflowing from under the tree. I couldn't leave Bob's side and asked Damon and Jenny and Ellen if they would help Kyra with her presents. It wasn't like me to have no energy for the celebration of Christmas and not enjoy watching everyone having fun, but it was seriously the last thing I wanted to do. I've heard Kyra say that was the worst Christmas ever.

After a few hours of hanging onto Bob's every breath, I realized this could go on and on, so I wandered over to the living room and paid some attention to Kyra and everyone else who were opening gifts. The day wore on and we eventually put dinner together as the community hadn't signed up for bringing us a meal. There was such an eerie feeling that evening in the house. Even though Bob didn't die on Christmas, he definitely seemed closer than ever to making his transition.

The next day we went back to the regular routine and I didn't feel as anxious, sensing his dying process could go on indefinitely. We didn't want visitors anymore and preferred to be together in our close family bubble.

Another day passed. I sat by his bed most of that day. His breathing was still irregular and I just wanted to be near him. I could look out the sliding glass windows just past his bed at the winter sky streaked with grey ribbons of clouds, and at the trees that were almost void of leaves, except for a few that fiercely hung on, much the way Bob was still holding onto life. I could see the pond that also was murky and dark due to the mostly overcast sky. Hilary was there and sat on the other side of Bob's bed. Mathieu, Ellen, and Jenny were on the couch watching TV just a few feet away.

Then it happened… he didn't take another breath. That moment we had been waiting in vigil for was finally here. It almost seemed anticlimactic. We announced it to the kids who were nearby but unaware. Mathieu came over, but the girls were giggling about something unrelated. They had heard my pronouncement like other times I had spoken, "I think this is it."

But I reiterated, "Girls, he has died."

They finally got it and came over to his bedside. It was Thursday, December 27th, 2001, at 8:15 pm, and it was surreal.

I called Hospice. Ellen went into a state of disbelief, said she had to leave, and went over to the neighbor's house. Jenny became very quiet and called Damon. Mathieu looked stunned, but also had a look of relief on his face. Someone called Chris.

Next I called the mortuary. I'd made these same calls hundreds of times for patients, but this time I felt numb and robotic. Our wonderful nurse, Susan, prepared Bob's body for pickup and cleaned up the medical "workspace" of all the supplies so that I wouldn't have to do this. Although it is a nurse's job to do these sorts of tasks, I will be forever grateful for the kindness she infused them with. She stayed until the Hospice Medical Social Worker, Mary, made a visit.

Mary had been a guardian angel for the kids. When she came to be with them, it was their time with her. No other adults participated so they had a safe place to talk about their feelings. We were so happy she could be with us that last lonely evening as we waited for the people from the funeral home to arrive.

I felt a bit ungrounded as this bearing-down weight was lifted from me. Helping your loved one die is in a way like giving birth. It is painful, labor intensive, and when it's over, you don't quite know what to do with yourself; there isn't a baby to hold like when you give birth. I had a shot of brandy to calm my nerves and so I didn't feel all of the emptiness.

The tears didn't come until much later.

Finally, an unmarked white van came to retrieve Bob's body. I walked out with them and watched as they put him into the back of the van. I knew it wasn't really him anymore, but I wanted to honor the body that had carried his amazing soul through this life.

Chris arrived just after the van left. He had passed the white van on his way down the street, sensing it contained his dad. We all reminisced around the table with Mary for a while longer.

The next day my friend, Robin, came over to help me compose an obituary for the paper. My Mom came over too, bringing food and making meals for us. In the living room, videos of Bob were being played all day. It was consoling to see him full of life in those videos, instead of how his body had wasted away over the previous six weeks. We felt his presence so strongly with us that day.

Over the next few days we planned the memorial service for January 6th. Mathieu had to go back to school, and the rest of the kids had to get back to their lives. The house that had held us all so close during those last six weeks was be-coming too big for Kyra and I, and it was really difficult for just me to keep two wood stoves going strong enough to warm up the place, yet I didn't want to leave right away. There was so much to be done before I could move back into my house.

Each of the children took a precious remembrance their Dad had wanted them to have. For Mathieu it was the chess set he had sculpted out of metal and the wooden table Bob had made. Jenny received the coffee table he had constructed of wood and tile. Chris had been given the dining room table that Bob had also made. Ellen's handmade gift from Bob was a wooden jewelry holder. Kyra would get the jewelry box that looked like a small table, which Bob originally had made for his mom.

Kyra couldn't quite fathom that this was all that was left of her relationship with her dad. I took her to weekly counseling sessions with a child therapist she had been seeing all through Bob's illness. She got through to Kyra's psyche via sand tray therapy, as talk therapy doesn't work with children. They have to "play" out whatever they are experiencing on an emotional or psychological level.

Hospice of the Foothills offered a children's art program to help those who have lost someone close to them, so I en-rolled Kyra. She worked through clay and painting modalities to express her grief. It never seemed that Kyra was feeling or expressing all of the loss that I know she must have had inside. She had such a close connection to Bob. Al-most every night for most of her almost nine years with him he made sure she had her bath, playtime, and then a story; that was their time. He played the guitar and sang to her while she took a bath. They acted out children's stories like Jack and the Beanstalk, Snow White, and Beauty and the Beast. While I would make dinner, they often snuggled together in the hammock out on the deck. They were like two peas in a pod. I was her mom and nurtured her in other ways, but I would never be Bob; never be her Dad.

In the years since, Mathieu, Ellen, and Aunt Hilary, as she was called, has given Kyra extra nurturing and personal time as I continued being a single parent. Other parents in Kyra's classes took her on trips and did fatherly activities with her, like teaching her how to fish etc. It does take a village to raise a child, and the universe continued to support us in the effort to give Kyra what she needed to become a successful young woman.

In a personal growth seminar I attended in my 30's, I learned that as human beings we really want to contribute to the well-being of others, but if the person you are trying to give to doesn't open up to receive the gift, the contribution can't be given. Even though Bob's dying was difficult for my family, and me it was made so much easier through the contributions from our families and community. This experience taught me it was so much bigger than I could possible handle on my own. I had to open up and receive all the good that wanted to be contributed by others: from the early on offers to sit and wait with me in the hospital through Bob's surgeries; the rides to radiation treatments for Bob; the meals from the community; the play dates for Kyra; the holiday dinners so lovingly cooked; the unending support from Hilary and Lynn, and the support from our engineering business employees and the local engineering firm of Holdrege and Kull. The list could go on and on.

By opening up to all of this good, it created an upward spiral of energy that showered the givers and us, the receivers, with love and appreciation. I believe that everyone got a gift from this special time.

Where in your life can you open up to all the good that wants to come your way? "Go-it-alone" leadership is exhausting. Where can you transition from being a lone wolf

leader and co-create a life/project/business that is all that you have ever wanted?

Chapter Six

"Life only demands from you the strength you possess."
– Dag Hammarskjold

**Message Six:
Even in the midst of chaos and confusion,
stay grounded.
Your strength assists others to find their own.**

You know you are in a crisis when too much is coming at you too fast. Like a plate spinner in the circus, if you can't keep all the plates spinning fast enough, some or all will fall, crash to the floor, and break into pieces. That is, unless, you remember to keep breathing and stay focused. From this place of powerful calm you become the peaceful eye in the center of the storm and make the right choices for you and all concerned. Here's how I did this.

"I'm in the hospital, Mom", Ellen said. "I overdosed on aspirin."

For a moment I stopped breathing. My eyes widened and every bump in the painted texture on the white kitchen wall popped out at me. My eyes traced the grain in the brown wooden windowsill. Slanted beams of light poured through the sliding glass door and landed on the brick red tile floor. I leaned into the wall as blood pulsed in my ears and a chill raced up my back.

Was this a bad dream?

When a memory surfaced that this wasn't the first time Ellen had made a suicide attempt, I came back to reality. I breathed with relief that she had called. A slight calming energy eased through my tight shoulders. It was late August1998 when I got this call. Ellen was twenty years old.

"I'm going to a separate place where they want to help me and maybe give me some medicine so I'm not so depressed."

Was this 'separate place' a mental health facility?"

I'm so happy to hear you are okay and that you're get-ting the care you need. Is there anything I can do to help right now?"

"Happy" was a lie. The back of my throat burned from rising stomach acid. My breaths were shallow. I held a stiff pose against the wall. For her, I pretended to be "happy," to let her know she and her life mattered to me and to keep her from hearing the fear in my voice.

"Could you come up here, Mom? They want you to be involved in my treatment."

"Of course I'll come up."

I was wondering how I could be there for both Ellen and Bob. He was getting chemotherapy and radiation treatments for colon cancer while keeping our engineering business going. Bob needed my support. So did Kyra, our very active four-year-old, whose care mostly fell to me. Now three people needed me, and there was only one of me.

I prayed to Spirit and quickly got into action. I arranged childcare for Kyra, made a hotel reservation near the hospital in Chico, shopped for food for Bob and Kyra, and then packed my suitcase and car. This activity helped me focus and stay grounded.

Finally, I put my hand on the door handle of the car and paused. My right foot felt like a lead weight as I placed it on the floorboard. Next I lowered my hips onto the driver's seat with my left foot still on the gravel carport driveway. I took another deep breath and slowly lifted that foot into the car and closed the door.

As I backed out, a pang of guilt coursed through me. It seemed I was abandoning someone no matter what I did. I prayed again, this time that my presence with Ellen would help her get the treatment she needed, and that Bob and Kyra would be okay. With rigid shoulders and hands tightly gripping the steering wheel, I pulled out of the drive way.

When I had settled into my hotel room in Chico, I called Ellen and she told me the psychiatrist wanted to meet with me. Ellen had been transferred to a locked facility next to the hospital.

As soon as I saw Ellen, her pale face and the frail, dazed look in her eyes alarmed me. We sat in a small, beige painted room with wood framed chairs covered with brown woven upholstery fabric. After introductions were made, the psychiatrist asked to interview me alone about Ellen's past.

I told him that five years earlier, about a month before I delivered Kyra, Ellen had attempted suicide. One morning she sheepishly walked in our bedroom before school looking ghostly and troubled, saying she needed to tell us some-thing.

"I took a half a bottle of aspirin during the night."
"Oh my God!"

I sucked in a huge breath, held it, and then jumped out of bed as fast as an eight-month pregnant woman can, blowing out that breath through pursed lips.

"Get your jacket on. We need to take you to the hospital."

I clenched my teeth as I threw on the maternity clothes that were getting tight. Why this? Why now? I was a nurse trained to show compassion in a crisis. Did I show Ellen some compassion in this moment? My sights had been on the birth of the baby growing in my body, a long awaited dream of mine to have one more child. Ellen obviously needed more from me. Maybe she was feeling jealous of this baby that was about to be born and fearful of losing me again. She had lost my full attention six years earlier when she was nine and I married Bob. Maybe she felt like she would lose all of me this time.

Ellen and I had been extremely close before I married Bob. My relationship with her birth father, Angelo, disintegrated while I was pregnant with her. I had hoped our marriage would improve after Ellen's birth, but it didn't. We separated before her first birthday and divorced when she was two. I was a single mother for years until Bob and I got together. Bob had three children from two previous marriages, and we had been married for five years before I be-came pregnant. My dream was to bring a child into an intact family where not just this child, but also all of our children knew they were loved. I felt a deep ache in my heart with Ellen's bold attempt to take her life. She was showing me she wasn't feeling included in this dream.

I had also been depressed as a teen and contemplated suicide. At sixteen, I thought my life was over because I had-not experienced love with a boyfriend. Wanting to be loved and cared for was a deep need; deep enough for me to want to end my life because I thought I would never find it. The only thing that kept me from following through was that I knew how much my parents loved me and how heartbroken they would be if I died. Money was tight in our family of six: two parents and four children. Feeling so depressed one day, I managed to look up the number for a psychiatrist, but I couldn't dial it. I didn't know how to pay for a visit to him. I couldn't ask for the support I needed and had to search inside myself to find it.

As preposterous as this seems, it never occurred to me that Ellen's earlier suicide attempt was the beginning of a bigger mental disorder. I assumed the earlier attempt was an adolescent impulse like I had experienced. I felt devastated to be eight months pregnant and watch my vibrantly healthy teenage daughter have a huge tube put down her throat. This tube would suction out the black charcoal mixture the ER nurse had given her to drink to absorb the harmful effects of the handfuls of aspirin she had ingested. Maybe the toxins could be removed, but I knew that hose couldn't suck out the sadness she was feeling. I silently wished some magical vacuum could suck away my own grief as I sat beside her. Emergency room staff hovered around her performing necessary medical procedures. There seemed to be a place in her that needed all of that attention. I vowed in that moment to find other ways to give her the love and care she needed.

We found a counselor for Ellen to explore why she felt suicide was her only option. Counseling gave her a new sense of herself. We also offered her registration in the Teen Forum, a weekend seminar led by Landmark Education. This helped her to discover more of her life purpose, and afterwards it was easier to talk with her about what was important to her.

Once Kyra was born, Ellen instantly became a doting big sister. She was so sweet with her, and enjoyed holding and playing with her.

When she turned sixteen, Ellen started dating a boy named Ken. They developed a close relationship and it seemed like she was living a normal teenage life. We stayed aware of her comings and goings and made sure she was keeping her agreements about completing her homework and chores. When she didn't, there were consequences, but for the most part her life was going well. She graduated from high school and was looking forward to going to college.

I could tell she was apprehensive the day we took her to Sonoma State University. As we walked by the other dorm rooms, students were busy decorating their rooms and claiming them as their own. We carried in Ellen's boxes, but she didn't make a move to open them and unpack. I suggested we make her bed with her new green plaid sheets and bedding—the extra-long kind specifically made for skinny dorm beds. I remembered being so excited to finally see my parents leave when they had dropped me off at my college dorm years before. However, Ellen's forehead was furrowed and her arms were wrapped tightly across her chest. She didn't seem to be excited for us to leave. I hoped her feelings would change and she would like living on her own, making friends, and becoming immersed in her education.

I noticed Ellen was coming home often on weekends. It was a three-hour trip from Sonoma State University to our home in the Sierra Nevada Mountains. I wondered why she wasn't more engaged with her peers.

Ellen had been a college-prep, advanced placement student in high school, so Bob and I were shocked when she didn't fulfill the requirements to stay in the Hutchins Pro-gram at Sonoma State, a special liberal arts program. She said she was having trouble reading. This didn't make sense. She had always been a good reader.

In hindsight, I can see why she had not been invited back after her freshman year. But I was disappointed. The money was one thing; we'd paid thousands of dollars on her college education with little to show for it. She was in a special program and if you didn't complete it, although the units were transferable, they wouldn't count for core classes. She would have to start college from the beginning again.

This was Ellen's first big failure. As she moved from the dorms to a rental house near Sonoma State, she said she hoped to return to college at some point. I delivered her bed from home and was surprised to see how insipid her skin looked, even in the middle of summer. Her clothes fit tighter and she didn't look me in the eye when we spoke.

She called home in tears often that summer. We listened and reassured her on every call. Bob went through another operation related to his cancer surgery and tried to comfort her by saying, "Sometimes life is hard, but somehow you get through it."

Before summer's end, she attended a camp in Vermont focusing on Global Leadership for Youth. She had been nominated to this camp by our friend, Steve Blumenthal, from The Hunger Project. The year before Ellen had pledged $5000 to The Hunger Project. Focus on this could have been another reason she wasn't successful in college. At eighteen years old, Ellen was the youngest person in its history to make and fulfill such a large pledge. She had traveled to New York and participated in conferences with people from all over the world, and had inspired so many with her commitment to end world hunger. At the time this seemed inspiring to us, but was this sign of mental illness known as "manic" or grandiose thinking? Steve had heard about her situation and wanted to support her to keep moving forward as the inspiring leader and visionary he had witnessed in the previous year.

Unbeknownst to us, Ellen was developing depression that summer and it got worse when she was in Vermont. She had little interest in the camp activities and had difficulty eating and sleeping.

When she came back to California, she moved back home, trying to figure out what to do next. She got a job at a local bakery, riding a bike to work, as she no longer had a car. One day that winter she walked in the house, wet from head to toe, sneakers squeaking and squirting water every step on the red tile in the kitchen?"

What happened to you?"

"Got caught in a downpour," she mumbled as she slogged into her room and shut the door like any teenager trying to get mom off her back. It was raining outside.

Two years later, when Ellen thought I could handle hearing the truth about this event, she told me she had ridden her bike deep down into the river canyon, to the raging Yuba River rapids and jumped in. She was wrong about my being able to hear what she was saying now. I could see her lips moving and see the trust in her big, dark brown eyes, but I couldn't hear anything. I stopped breathing and cupped my hand over my gaping mouth. My stomach muscles tightened and a cold chill ran down my chest and into my stomach. I was holding back a panicky swirl of nerves that made my headache and my mouth dry and sticky. Gulping down the horror of this scene, I pushed a scream down hard into my belly. I wanted to turn away from visualizing her body being tossed about by the rapids and her arms flailing as if I was turning away from a horrifying movie, but I couldn't do that. If I did, surely she would think I was shunning this act, shunning her.

"How did you get out alive?"

"The water was icy cold, so cold I couldn't breathe. The rapids kept pushing me under water."

My own breaths became shorter and shallower. With eyes frozen wide open, I kept looking right at her as I made the journey from this bizarre nightmare to being present with her in this moment.

"As soon as I jumped in, something in my body took over. I still wanted to die, but my body didn't. It fought hard to survive and got me to the shore, and I somehow pulled myself out."

I let out a big sigh and drew her close to me, feeling her every breath, my heart aching for her anguish.

Even without knowing this, I had noticed how Ellen's gaze turned downwards more often than it met my eyes, and how her shoulders were far too hunched over for a nine-teen year old person. Previously I had brought home a brochure about how the herb, St. John's Wort, could help depression and suggested she take it. In a few weeks of doing so, her mood lifted.

Heidi, a good friend of Ellen's from high school, had moved to Chico in December of 1997. After visiting her for a couple of weeks, Ellen decided to move there in January of1998. She started living with her half-brother, Mathieu, and signed up to attend Butte Junior College. Still not having a car, she took a bus to school and rode a bike around town. Making peace with her past and with a fresh start, she registered for astronomy and ceramics classes, and got a job at the Butte College TV station. This job ended at the close of the spring semester. Her time living with Mathieu was ending as he had graduated from high school and was going to LA to attend college.

We told Ellen if she wasn't going to college and was living away from home, she would have to pay her own expenses. She rented an apartment, found a roommate, and got a delivery job with the Chico Bread Company.

"Mom, I can't wait to show you my new apartment," she said when we attended Mathieu's graduation party.

We drove over to take a look. As we walked down the stairway with dark brown wall paneling, the apartment smelled musty and dank. The rooms in the apartment had strangely low ceilings and only a few high windows letting in little light. It looked like a dungeon to me. I didn't under-stand her choice, but I hoped it was right for her. Bob had been diagnosed with colon cancer the month prior and our focus were now on his treatment.

I later learned Ellen was still severely depressed before she moved to Chico. She had made another attempt to end her life by sitting in the car in our garage at our home in Nevada City with the door closed and the engine running. Thankfully, the garage was not airtight and this attempt was also unsuccessful. She told me her high-school friend, Cathy, and she had talked about other ways they could both be successful at ending their lives.

It was just a few months after seeing her apartment when I received the call that Ellen was in the hospital after her fourth suicide attempt. As I sat in the room being inter-viewed by her doctor in the locked psychiatric facility, he told me that although Ellen hadn't exhibited many signs of manic behavior, they were leaning toward a diagnosis of Bipolar Disorder, formerly known as Manic Depression.

Ellen later confided that this previous summer had been a continual downward spiral. She had moved into the "dungeon" apartment, and although she had a job, she didn't make enough money to pay for everything. With Bob's colon cancer and our statement that she had to make her own way, she didn't feel she could ask for any help.

"I only ate once a day. It was too overwhelming to go in a grocery store and figure out what to buy, and then follow through on cooking and cleaning and everything. The whole process was too much so I just stayed away from them.

"My heart sunk. "I so wished I had known."

"I felt like you had too much on your mind with Bob's cancer."

"I know, honey, but I always want you to feel like you can call and talk to me…about *anything*. That's what a mother is for!"

Her working hours were bizarre. On Sundays, she started at three a.m. to drive up to the Redding Farmer's Market, and couldn't sleep the night before.

On that summer day, August 26, 1998, at the farmer's market where she sold bread, she told me that she noticed everything looked "grey" and didn't have any color. It was as if she was in a waking dream where she saw people walking by shopping for their produce—people who had lives, families, and a sense of purpose to their day. They seemed to be doing well, but she felt separate, alone, and excluded. With an overwhelming sense of doom, she told herself that she was cursed to live a life where nothing worked out for her. On her drive back to Chico, she stopped at a drug store and bought an economy size bottle of 500 tablets of aspirin. In her despair, she had forgotten that her earlier attempt with aspirin didn't give her the final results she was after. Or maybe subconsciously she did remember and knew she wouldn't really die, but was again crying out for help.

Her friend, Cathy, had come over that evening to watch a video. Without Cathy knowing, Ellen went into the other room and nonchalantly ingested handfuls of the aspirin, al-most half of the bottle.

Ellen began feeling sleepy. Cathy sweetly "tucked" her in and went back to her own apartment. Now alone in the "dungeon" apartment, Ellen slumbered half awake, waiting to die. A fear or survival instinct aroused her within a few hours as she started feeling shaky and "weird." She called her friend, Betsy.

"I did something stupid. Can you take me to the hospital?"

In the months leading up to this, the Chico Bread Company was having difficulties keeping their business operating. Ellen had come home to visit during that time. I remember her full of energy, tanned, yet thin. The winter before when she had been experiencing depression, she was sluggish and had gained a lot of weight. Her tanned and toned body and enthusiastic statements deceived me that she was finding her stride and taking responsibility for her-self as an independent young adult.

"I think I should become President of Chico Bread and make it a success!"

In a family of "big" thinkers, it was not uncommon for one of us to blurt out statements of a possibility like this. For me it was a sign that Ellen's spirit was coming alive and her spunk and determination were returning. Sitting in this locked mental facility I was learning this, instead, was a sign of mania.

As the psychiatrist said "mania," my mouth dropped and I took a slow, shallow breath. I held it a long time be-fore it slowly eked out of my mouth, over my dry tongue and out my lips. My thoughts drifted to what I had learned about mania in nursing school; about how people with mania spent large sums of money in a short period of time, stayed awake without sleeping for days, talked rapidly about unbelievable ideas, and didn't eat regular meals. A pattern was emerging here. Why hadn't I seen it?

This doctor prescribed Depakote, a seizure medication that worked well for young people diagnosed with Bipolar Disorder (BPD) in controlling their symptoms, but did not have the bad liver and kidney side effects that the standard Lithium treatment had. Unfortunately, he said it would take many weeks for the medication to take effect.

"Would you like to stay here in Chico while you learn how to manage your Bipolar Disorder and wait to feel better?" I asked.

Ellen shrugged her shoulders, looking down at the brown variegated carpet in the counselor's office.

"Would you like to come home and let the medications take effect?"

"No."

"I'm wondering how you will take care of yourself."

"I don't have a job anymore."

"Maybe your new job is to take care of you."

"I don't want to leave Chico."

"I could stay with you for a while to help you with meal planning and shopping."

Once she was released from the locked facility, we went back to her dungeon apartment. We walked down the dark brown paneled stairway. With each step, the stale, dusty, dank smell got stronger. The low ceilings and dark rooms with little daylight felt tomblike. I wondered how anyone with depression could feel better living here.

I had been reminded time after time while she was in the hospital that Ellen was twenty. She was legally an adult, and even though I was her parent, I had no authority over her. I could not access her health information nor could I make any decisions for her. Our laws say at eighteen a person has the legal rights of an adult, but in reality few eighteen-year-olds have the skills needed to live as a fully functioning adult. Regardless, I knew the only hope for her becoming a healthy adult lay in empowering her to make good choices for herself.

As Ellen's disorder had progressed, she had increasing difficulty in shopping and cooking for herself. This was the first skill we took on.

"Mom, it is just too confusing when I go into a store. I can't decide what to eat or buy."

During our first days out of the hospital, I suggested ways she could bring more balance to her life. We bought a kitchen table so she would have a place to prepare and eat her meals. Next we went shopping and bought ingredients for easy to cook healthy meals.

After several days of helping her create a healthy lifestyle, her depression was not improving. I knew the doc-tor said it could take weeks for her meds to kick in, but I felt an aching pull to get back to the rest of my family and home. Ellen's birth father hadn't spent much time with her as she grew up due to our divorce, but she had lived with him for part of her senior year and they were on good terms. I suggested she go visit him in Arcata, on the beautiful coast of Northern California, as she waited for her meds to take effect. Nothing sounded good to her, but she agreed to go. I thought anything was better than sitting in that dungeon apartment. Her dad was able to get her an economical car, which boosted her self-esteem and sense of empowerment.

After a few weeks visiting with her father, Ellen came back to her apartment in Chico and was still depressed, but was taking her meds. Her anxiety level was increasing so she drove down to see her grandmother who lived near us. One day during her visit, my mom called me to say there was something wrong with Ellen.

"She has been sitting in the bedroom staring out the window and not moving for hours," she said,

"I'll be right down."

Clenching my teeth, I slammed the phone down. I panicked and took off at a run, but in two steps, stopped, turned around and ran back to the phone. My pulse was racing and I was already out of breath. I rapidly pecked out the numbers to Bob's cell phone.

"Bob, I need you to come home right now. Ellen is acting really strange and staring off into space at my Mom's. I have to get down there. Please come be with Kyra."

I tossed the phone in the cradle and raced up the first half-flight of slippery tiled stairs, almost sliding sideways as I made the right-hand turn to go up the other half-flight. I ran down the ivory and brown speckled carpet to our bedroom, threw a few days' worth of clothes, pajamas, and toiletries in an overnight case, and tore out of the room. I heard Bob opening the front door as I was running down the stairs, passing him as I went out without even a kiss or hug goodbye Kyra. Mommy loves you," I yelled over my shoulder.

"I'll call you when I know something," I hollered out to Bob, who was waving goodbye. The tires made a crunching sound on the gravel driveway as I hurriedly backed out, leaving a cloud of dust as I sped forward onto the street.

A steady vibration of energy raced up and down my arms, legs, and torso, sending waves of pressure into my head as I made the 30-minute drive down to my Mom's. My breaths were shallow and fast, my nostrils flaring as they re-leased the air from my lungs.

When I got there, I didn't bother to knock on my Mom's front door. I walked fast over the tan carpet down the hall to the spare bedroom, my flip-flops slapping my heels hard. I turned into the bedroom and saw Ellen sitting rigidly on the bed, staring out the sliding glass door, unaware I had entered the room. I have since learned this is called depression psychosis. I quietly eased onto the bed next to her, like you would approach an injured animal.

"I'm here, Ellen. It's your Mom. Tell me what is going on."

Her eyelids make a half-blink, but her lips stayed tightly closed.

"I'm going to get some help for you."

I thought she could hear me, couldn't she?

My breaths felt even shallower as I walked out of the bedroom, noticing the sun was low in the sky. Hot energy kept moving through my body. My chest felt tight. There wasn't much time left in the business day. My shoulders and neck muscles squeezed tighter.

"Can I use your phone, Mom? I've got to find help for Ellen immediately."

My mouth felt dry and my throat tightened as I dialed the phone, first calling my former colleague, Ricky, who was a Licensed Clinical Social Worker (LCSW) and has experience with mental illness. After Ellen's recent hospitalization, I had called her, asking general questions about BPD and if she thought we were on the right track. Now I was asking if she had a daughter with Ellen's current symptoms, what she would do. She said she would take her to Langley Porter Psychiatric Institute in San Francisco.

I called this institute right away and discussed Ellen's symptoms. They said I could make an appointment and bring her in for an exam by one of their psychiatrists. I said I felt it was an emergency considering her current state and wanted to get her help right away. I asked if I brought her to the ER of UCSF hospital if they would admit her to the Langley Porter Institute and they said if she was suicidal, they probably would. Ellen's father, Angelo, earned more major points with me because he had kept Ellen on his insurance policy. I called the number on the back of the card and they said her policy covered visits to UCSF.

"Halleluiah!"

I let out a huge sigh and finally felt my feet on the floor. As I went back to Ellen's bedroom, I felt more myself and told her we had to drive to San Francisco because this was where the best help for her was located. She slowly walked with me to the car and we made the three-hour drive from Auburn to San Francisco.

Unfortunately, I was leaving Bob and Kyra once again. To help them in my absence, I called some friends. This was becoming such a nightmare for me. Would it ever end? I called my friend, Deborah, who lived in San Francisco, and she said I could stay with her if Ellen were admitted to the hospital.

I drove into the ER of UCSF and helped Ellen to the waiting room. The MD who saw her had square, thick black-framed glasses, black straight hair, and deep creases gouging his face from the sides of his nose down past his mouth. He asked Ellen the question I was both waiting for and dreading.

"Have you thought of taking your life?"

"Yes."

"Do you have a plan?"

"Yes."

"Well, I am going to admit you to the hospital."

I breathed shallowly as I stared at the speckled grey linoleum floor. I couldn't look at Ellen. Even as her mother, this seemed too intimate of a conversation to witness, some-thing no one ever wants to admit. The energy raced in my body even more and I longed to escape from this small white painted room. I never wanted these questions to be asked of my family, or me but today was one of those increasingly bizarre days I was living through. I wished I'd never heard my child's answers. I wondered what "plan" Ellen had to end her life.

Even though anxious feelings had coursed through my body all day, I was able to tap into a place of strength and calm. The belief that Spirit never gives me more than I can handle was a silent mantra and I was drawing on the power that is greater than me that day.

In just a few minutes they wheeled her up to the seventh floor and buzzed her into the locked ward. They told me to come back tomorrow. I quickly hugged and kissed her be-fore she disappeared behind the thick heavy brown door. Surrendering into the wheelchair, she blankly stared for-ward, not responding to my embrace. I jumped when the door slammed with a loud clang and a thud.

Would she find the safety, treatment, and comfort she needed behind those locked doors?

There is strength greater than you possess that you can tap into at any time to stay grounded. By staying centered you can access the wisdom you have to meet any challenge.

Chapter Seven

*"Sometimes the things we can't change
end up changing us instead."*
–Unknown

**Message Seven:
Allow what you cannot change to transform you
so that you become the person you were meant to be.**

I found my way to my friend Deborah's home in the Haight-Ashbury section of San Francisco. Deborah has such an enormous heart. It felt so good to sink into it and be held by her love. This was a scary time for me on so many levels. I felt I was abandoning Bob and Kyra while trying to help Ellen. Bob was sick from the side effects of chemo, and Kyra was probably scared to see her Daddy so sick. Now Mommy was away from home, but when your first-born is staring into space and thinking of committing suicide, that trumps everything. I had to be there for Ellen and prayed my com-munity would support Bob and Kyra. Our babysitter, Janet, would be there for Kyra. Another friend and business partner, Baker, was there for Bob, taking him to radiation every day and helping keep the business going with him. I felt so much gratitude for their support.

The next day I went to visit Ellen. It was a gloomy, overcast, drizzly late summer day in San Francisco. Just a month ago she had been released from the psychiatric facility in Chico. I went up to the locked door where I had said good-bye the night before. I pushed the white rectangular button on the silver intercom speaker.

A monotone sounding voice said, "Hello. How can I help you?"

"I'm Ellen Frudakis' mother, here to visit her."

"Hold on," the voice said, sounding as if I was bothering her.

A loud buzz sounded and the uninviting voice said, "You can come in."

I pushed the heavy brown door open and walked in, my feet slowly moving on shiny white linoleum squared floors scattered with black and grey scuff marks. A large room with white walls and black lounge-type furniture opened up to the right. I saw a few middle-aged people wearing vacant expressions sitting on the furniture. I didn't see Ellen anywhere, so I went up to the nurses' station and asked where she was. They pointed me to her room.

Her small room had white walls and floors and was sparsely furnished. She sat on her bed covered with white sheets and a charcoal-colored wool blanket, hugging her knees and looking lost and withdrawn. I wrapped my arms around her unresponsive body then sat back on the cold tan metal folding chair.

"How is it going here, honey?"

"Okay."

"Have they started you on any new medications?"

"I don't know."

"Have you seen the psychiatrist?" I asked, pressing for any info that would help relieve my angst.

"I think so," she slowly answered.

I was relieved she was at least speaking to me, but she mostly mumbled and didn't really seem to be aware of what was going on.

"Are you glad you are here now?" I guardedly asked, hoping for a yes.

"I guess," she said with a flat voice.

"Want to go for a walk?"

I needed to get out of her small room and see what the environment and people were like. My daughter was now held captive with them.

We walked back to the open room where there were games, puzzles, and a TV. I asked her if she wanted to play a game. We settled on checkers. It was eerily quiet and all you could hear was the tapping of the checkers on the board. When we were done, she just wanted to go back to her room and lie on her bed. I told her I would come back the next day.

I went out to the nurse's station and asked how she was doing.

"We're sorry, but your daughter is over eighteen so we can't tell you anything."

I felt my face flush. How many times am I going to hear this?

"She is seeing the psychiatrist, isn't she?" I pleaded for more information.

"All of our patients see their doctors," she answered flippantly.

"Can I get his phone number?"

She scribbled it on a piece of paper.

It felt so strange to leave this unit, have the door slam hard and lock behind me. Had I brought her to the right place? Was she getting the help she needed? I hadn't seen any young people here. Was there a better place I could have taken her to? I had heard this was the best place for treatment. Was she really safe here? Would she ever be able to find herself again?

How could my girl get so lost? How did this happen? I called Angelo to tell him what was going on with our daughter. He couldn't seem to grasp the situation and wouldn't make the trip to see her. We had divorced when she was a baby. His infrequent visits with her hadn't fostered a strong relationship between them. As a single mom, I had always picked up the pieces. *Couldn't he tell this was too big a piece for me to pick up this time?*

I felt a heavy pressure in my chest and couldn't take a deep breath. My neck felt tight and sore. This was another bad dream.

I called my mom. She planned to drive down with her sister, my Aunt Dot, and visit Ellen. Finally, I felt a little comfort. I could always count on my mom and aunt to come through for me.

For days it seemed all I did was waiting. Wait for visiting hours. Wait for permission to talk to what seemed to be phantom doctors. I finally spoke with Ellen's psychiatrist a few days into her stay. He had decided to switch her to Lithium since the Depakote wasn't working after a month's trial, and now she was experiencing a deepening depression. The doctor added an antidepressant to her treatment regimen. We discovered Ellen had Bipolar Disorder Type II, which meant her moods cycled between hypomania, a mild form of mania, and severe depression. I hoped Ellen would show signs of response soon.

As a Registered Nurse I worked in serious medical situations. Mental illness isn't treated like an acute illness. There is a lot of waiting involved. Even Bob's cancer treatment moved along faster! Fortunately I was developing a deeper empathy and compassion for patients and families going through similar situations.

I visited Ellen daily. One day she was working on a puzzle with another patient. Ellen seemed quite at home with this woman who was decades older and acted very withdrawn and anxious. I wondered again if Ellen was in the right environment. How could my baby girl belong here?

Many years later I asked Ellen about this. She told me the locked environment made her feel safe, as did being around other people that were dealing with similar diagnoses. It didn't matter what her fellow mental patients looked like on the outside, they understood what she was feeling on the inside.

One day while passing the time at Deborah's, I called my older brother, Tom, to tell him about Ellen.

"Well. You know this is your fault, don't you?"

Usually understanding and supportive, his voice became loud and angry as he blamed me for Ellen's situation.

My throat tightened and a pain seared down through my chest. Tom had been a brother I had looked up to. How could he say Ellen's diagnosis was my fault and not offer any empathy and kindness? My face was hot and beet red; I had tears in my eyes.

"She needed more from you as she was growing up."

My breathing stopped for a second as another pain went down my chest into my stomach. The back of my throat ached as I held back tears. I could never show my tears to my brothers growing up. I had to be brave or they would tease me with no mercy. The crying coupled with the teasing was humiliating for me.

"I'll talk to you later," I blurted out as I hung up the phone.

Speechless, I breathed hard to keep the tears from breaking through. As every parent who loves their child, I had done my best for Ellen. As a single, working mom, I did rely on childcare to fill in the gaps. Now faced with her mental illness that kept worsening, I had found what was purported to be the best mental facility in the area, maybe even in the country. Didn't he understand how heartbreaking this was for me? With all I was going through with Bob's illness and now Ellen's, couldn't he show some compassion? But Tom voiced the very darkest of my fears. *Was it my fault?*

When I shared with Deborah what my brother had said she told me to tell my brother to go "F" himself. I felt hurt and alone from my conversation with Tom, but didn't feel like confronting him. My husband Bob was so loving and reassuring, even with all he had going on, and I drew solace from that.

After many days of waiting and visiting Ellen once a day, I felt a compelling need to get back home. Other family and friends were scheduling visits with Ellen so she had additional support.

Ellen's psychiatrist, Dr. Cho, made it clear Ellen would not be able to return to her apartment in Chico. She would need to move back home with us.

While she stayed in the psychiatric facility and with Ellen's agreement, I went home to get a trailer, some boxes, and asked some friends to help me move her belongings. In Ellen's apartment we saw dirty dishes lining the sink, trash cans full and the laundry hamper overflowing with clothes. The refrigerator was empty. There was dust everywhere.

We brought boxes of all sizes into the small living room. It was unnerving to pack up someone else's things, even if it they were my daughter's. I wanted to look over my shoulder and explain to a formless energy why I was intruding here. Unnerving pulses of energy vibrated through my body. My dear friend, Robin, broke through my angst.

"Let's put little love notes inside all of the boxes. Someday when she unpacks her things they will make her smile."

I could feel my heartbeat slow as we penned "Angel Face, Bright Light, Leader, and Beautiful" and drew smiley faces and hearts on pieces of a yellow note pad and tucked them inside the cardboard boxes. Lastly, we taped and labeled the boxes with a black marker stating the contents within each of them. This gesture calmed my angst and transmuted it to sending love to a forthcoming vision of Ellen.

We made the round trip from Grass Valley to Chico and back in one day, unloading Ellen's boxes in our garage. Her young adult life and her dreams were now on hold.

I came home to find Bob wasn't doing so well with his cancer treatment. Diarrhea was causing him much pain. It had been difficult to be away from him as I was unable to give him any comfort from a distance except verbally. His doctor ordered a steroidal medication to reduce the diarrhea and pain. With his warrior spirit, Bob still got up every day, went to have his radiation treatments, and then worked in our engineering business.

Kyra had enough attention from family and friends that she seemed to be coping okay with all of the chaos in our family. I was so thankful she had such a strong spirit.

Ellen's psychiatrist, Dr. Cho, finally called and said it was time for her to be discharged, and I drove down to San Francisco to pick her up. She seemed a little less depressed and withdrawn. Dr. Cho said it would be best if she could attend a day treatment program.

We sought out whatever help was available in Nevada County where we lived, but the only counseling and support groups met infrequently. I also called Ricky again, who told me about a day treatment program in Auburn setup by Dr. Foster, a psychiatrist. He felt Ellen was a good match for his program. We took a tour of his facility and were pleased to see younger people attending the program. The therapist, Colleen, with short brown hair and a bubbly personality, was youthful and empowering. The treatment emphasized art therapy. That really excited Ellen. Frankly, I was thrilled to see her excited about anything!

Even though Ellen had been through so much in the previous two months, it felt like real support was surfacing that could actually help her heal. Being home all day waiting around for medicines to kick in would be hard for anyone, but especially for a young adult. I was anxious about her driving the sixty-mile round trip to this program every day, but I also felt hopeful she would start regaining her vitality, personality, and autonomy through this experience.

The first week Ellen came back to live with us, everyone felt uneasy.

"How did your day go?"

"Ugh."

"Did you get to do some art today?"

"No."

"Are you making any friends?"

Bob was screaming in pain upstairs. We both winced.

"I don't want to talk right now."

Ellen slammed the door.

I gave her a little breather and then went back to her room to talk to her.

"Can you give me any indication that this day treatment is helping you? I'd really like to know."

She glared at me and said an emphatic "NO!"

"With all I have done for you over the past two months, this is all you can give me?" Now I slammed the door as I walked out of her room.

A feeling of trepidation coursed through me in that moment. Bob continued to yell in pain from the upstairs bathroom. I knew this was not a good situation for either Bob or Ellen. They both needed a peaceful, supportive, environment for healing.

What was a better solution? All of a sudden my mom came to mind.

A year before, my father had passed away. After a fifty-four year marriage, my mom was still grieving his loss and feeling lonely. Ellen and my mom had always been close. I wondered if she would be willing to have Ellen stay with her for a while. I called her and told what was going on. Bob was yelling in pain and Ellen angry and withdrawn. I told her it felt like Ellen could use some distance from this situation to allow her to heal.

"Could she come stay with you?"

There was a pause in the conversation.

My eyes closed tight and my face screwed up. I held my breath as thoughts ricocheted in my head. *Please say yes. Oh, you won't say yes, this is too much to ask. Families are supposed to take care of their own. There's nothing wrong with me. I can handle this. Oh…please say yes!* "

Yes, I think that would work."

Every muscle in me relaxed.

"Bless you, Mom. This will really help everyone get what they need."

I went back to Ellen's room and told her my idea. She agreed, started packing her things, and drove down to her grandmother's. Sadness and relief washed over me. This wasn't my first choice, but it was best for the entire family.

I checked in often with Ellen. She drove to the treatment program every day, which was easier as her grandmother lived fifteen miles closer to the center. I worried about her driving on the curvy rural highways, but her medication change was slowly starting to work. Her bubbly personality started coming back. I had to tell myself it was okay for her to take on a more normal life.

She was introduced to a ceramic artist who volunteered at the day treatment center, and Ellen started coming alive through her work with clay. This artist invited her to be an intern in his private studio. She completed her treatment in six weeks and then started working solely for this artist. He had mentored many mentally ill people who had found healing through creativity. I had met him and felt Ellen would be safe and supported in an internship with him.

Ellen's artistic expression branched into painting. She had no formal training, but started buying canvases and be-came a prolific painter. She used broad strokes with brightly colored paint, often of whimsical human figures. They made you smile when you looked at them. At this point she was feeling better and Bob had completed his treatment and was recovering, too, so Ellen came back to live with us.

During the winter she lived with us, Ellen got to a point where she wasn't getting better and was still experiencing some depression. Watching television, working on puzzles, and having companionship with her grandmother had helped, and the painting was also therapeutic.

By the springtime, she completed her internship with the ceramicist. She found a summer program for artists at the San Francisco Academy of Art. It cost several thousand dollars and included dorm residency. Bob always wanted our children to pay for a portion of the things or experiences that they wanted in their lives rather than having us fund the total cost. Ellen decided to have an auction of the art items she had been making. She invited friends and family and sold almost every piece. Everyone was delighted with his or her art pieces and many still have them on display in their homes. She easily made her goal of half of her tuition. It was so inspiring to see her taking on her life again.

We drove her down to her dorm in the Pacific Heights area of San Francisco in June, 1999. What a difference from dropping her off at college two summers before. During the past year she had lost her way, but now she was on a new and powerful journey. She would have to get herself to her classes in locations all over San Francisco by using public transportation. It was uncanny that less than a year before she had been in a locked mental facility and now she was freely traveling around San Francisco, experiencing life and creativity as never before. She even developed some friend-ships that have lasted to this day.

At the end of the program at the Academy of Art, she met a gallery owner from Davis, California, and was able to get a job working for him. She found an apartment, this time an upstairs one with lots of light. It felt like the light had come on in her soul again as she made this new start. I helped her move the boxes that we had packed up in Chico. Ellen was moving forward again as an adult living on her own with new roommates in a new town.

One day shortly after she had moved, I got a call from her.

"Mom! I found the adorable notes you put in the boxes!"

"Oh my gosh, I had forgotten about those! That was Robin's idea."

"I feel so happy now, Mom."

"When we were writing those notes, Elle, you were in such a dark place. Those notes really helped me, too, as they helped me to see you in a happier time. Now, here you are!"

"I know, Mom. I am feeling so much better. Thank you for thinking positive thoughts back then. I think they helped me get here."

We came to several art gallery openings Ellen hosted. Her work at the gallery inspired her to enter some of her own art in a few contests. She felt a pull to the artist community in Sacramento and eventually got a job at another gallery. There were paintings and metal sculptures featured in this gallery, and the metal sculptures foundry was located in the back of the building.

Ellen continued to paint, enjoyed making collages, and found art pieces. She lived in a Victorian house near downtown. Several times she would attempt to take a college class at the nearby community college, but after a few sessions she would drop out saying it was too difficult for her to keep the concentration and focus needed. During these years she lived in Davis and Sacramento I would get calls from her when she was really down and didn't know how to help herself. I would listen, offer suggestions, and communicate my love, reminding her she was stronger than she knew and she'd make it through these times.

Grief hit Ellen hard after Bob died at the end of 2001. I will always remember the evening I received a call from her in the summer of 2002. She was screaming and crying, and I could not understand what she was saying. Eventually she was able to calm herself and say that her younger half-brother, Evan, from her biological dad, had committed suicide. She had always suspected he had some form of mental illness, and this tragedy confirmed it. These two deaths led Ellen into a period of deep grief.

Earlier that spring in 2002, Ellen's friend, Erin, invited her to go to Santa Cruz. During this visit Ellen met a young man named Jonathan. He was raised in San Diego and invited Ellen to go visit his family there. I felt a flutter of fear run up my spine. This seemed risky to me, traveling across the state with someone she hardly knew. Even though this was an experience most young adults have as they start out on their own, I wasn't sure if Ellen was ready for so much independence. I wanted to share in her excitement, but I worried she was having some symptoms of mania.

On their visit to San Diego she fell in love with the area, with Jonathan, and especially with the weather. She learned quickly that the weather had a huge impact on her depression. Temperatures in the 70's and sunny skies made her immediately feel better. I hoped beyond hope that this would be the change Ellen needed to create a life she loved. I wanted to trust that this was a wise decision, but I noticed I held my breath whenever I thought about her moving. She would be so far away. Living in Sacramento, I could see her in an hours' drive. Now she would be living a full days' drive or a plane ride away.

How did I stay grounded through Ellen's four suicide attempts and bipolar diagnosis while helping my husband in his "dance" with cancer, and raising Kyra who was in her formative years from birth through age 8?

Maybe it was my experience as a registered nurse. When you work in a hospital, life has many tenuous and stressful moments. One minute you are speaking with a patient, then the next you are calling an emergency code, administering CPR, and working with the code team, yet also making sure the family's needs are met if they are visiting. It's a three-ring circus. Sometimes you have to cry with the sadness of it all; other times you console the family, move the patient to ICU, and before long a new patient is in that bed needing your care. As a nurse you get used to trauma and change.

Maybe it was just my nature to be able to stay calm with so many stressful events happening at once. My friends call me Mother Earth. I am a good listener and grounded by nature. I spend time every day connecting with the Divine source and I know when I am connected to that energy, all things are possible, especially being calm in a storm.

If it is true for me that I can find a sense of calm and peace in troubled times, then so can you. I can't tell you exactly how I do it, but I just stay focused and calm in the moment, and sense all the help I need is with me and this helps me get through the difficulty.

Maybe it is my faith that things tend to work out for the best that leads me through hard times. How was it the best that Bob died, that Ellen is diagnosed with mental illness, and that Kyra lost her beloved father? Well, as we all find out sooner or later in life, we don't have control over what happens, but we do have control over how we respond.

We all have a choice in how we view the trials and tests in life. I believe it is important to find the gifts in what hap-pens and use them to create what it is we want to have in our lives. I want love and family in my life. We lost an important member, but we moved forward and created a new form for our family. Ellen found the gifts in her bipolar diagnosis and created more of what she wanted in her life. We all became more of who we were meant to be.

As a leader, what do you not have control over? How is this transforming you to become all that you were meant to be?

Part Three

~

Shine Your Leadership Light and Make an Impact

Chapter Eight

*"One of the major keys to success is to
keep moving forward on the journey,
making the best of the detours and interruptions,
turning adversity into advantage.*
-John C. Maxwell

**Message Eight:
Keep Moving Forward With Inspired Action**

Ellen and Jonathan found a cute white Victorian apartment that overlooked downtown San Diego. Not long after settling in, she registered for a class in study habits for people with disabilities at the San Diego City College (SDCC).This got her involved with the Learning Resources Department. They educated her that BPD affected her experience of learning like any other learning disability, and that there were things they could do to help her with those challenges. The counselors showed great interest in her and helped her learn about available resources and what kind of learning style would assist her even with BPD.

One day she called me with so much excitement.

"Mom, I've found the college I want to go to. It's called Springfield College in Massachusetts, and they have a satellite campus here in San Diego. They use a seminar style learning approach. You don't sit in a lecture hall and listen to a professor; you sit at a round table facing one another and discuss the material with other students and the teacher."

"That is so wonderful. It sounds like more of a feminine style of learning."

"I know, and this college is also focused on community development, something else I'm interested in. I don't know yet exactly what I want to study, but I think I will discover it."

"This sounds so great for you, honey!"

As I said this I started tingling inside, feeling like a champagne bottle cork escaping its' tight bottleneck. I was wild with excitement that Ellen was releasing the tight hold BPD had on her life. She was finding her way back to her-self. She had been such a great student in high school. With all of her difficulties finding recovery for her BPD, I had al-most given up on the dream I had for her to graduate from college. But in this moment the dream was coming alive again.

"Oh, and Mom, the resource center at SDCC is helping me get grants through the Department of Rehab and I'm also applying for other financial aid. I think most of my tuition and book money will be covered."

"Wow, this sounds like it was meant to be!"

As she enrolled in Springfield, Ellen and Jonathan moved into a cottage. This college opportunity, the cottage, and her new life were opening up so fast I wondered if I was in a dream or if it really was a dream-come-true.

This style of learning was the right fit for Ellen. She thrived in an environment balancing mind, body, and spirit, both individually and in community. How uncanny it was that she would find a college program that would support her in finding balance while living with a BPD diagnosis. I knew in my heart that unseen forces were at work supporting her recovery.

Her professors challenged her and acknowledged her abilities and progress. She studied hard and made new friends. She continued to get support for her BPD with counseling, consistent medication management and by attending a support group.

Those frequent calls where she was crying and paralyzed by her BPD had stopped. She would still call and share tough moments, but we all have those types of days. She was able to navigate them with a sense of purpose. I was so in-spired by her!

The worry I had for her totally lifted. Now I could focus on being Kyra's mom and recreating my life since losing Bob. Ellen was teaching me to reawaken dreams for my life.

As Ellen entered her final year of undergraduate work, she was required to create a senior project. Remembering how much her BPD support group helped her find peers, she decided to focus on creating a group for young people with mental illness. She invited youth from The Meeting Place Clubhouse, a place for people with mental illness to get support and find community, to meet with her. Her friend, Johanna Baker, whom she had met there, agreed to participate as a co-founder.

In February of 2004, Ellen and Johanna held the first meeting. Together they brainstormed different ideas about the group they were creating. The members decided it would be focused on creating and having fun social activities. Many young adults with mental illness become isolated, having next to no social life. The members of this new group met weekly to plan their first event, a picnic at Balboa Park. This led to weekly planning meetings to discuss what other social activities they would do and when. Weekend trips to Sea World, bowling, movies, and miniature golf were the start of their fun together. Ellen figured they would do this until they discovered the true purpose of their group. They also came up with a name to call themselves: Impact Young Adults or IYA for short.

Fast forward to the graduation of the young woman who a few years earlier could only go to a small number of college classes before dropping out. Ellen was now earning a Bachelor of Arts in Human Services. She had reached a level of recovery from a mental illness that had at one time limited her ability to express herself and share her talents and gifts. She had accomplished a long dreamed goal. Every mother is proud at her child's college graduation, but my elation was indescribable. The sweetness of that hard-won feat had us grinning, as so many had hoped for this moment for Ellen. In a moment of surprise and delight, Ellen was honored with a special award called the Humanics Award. It is given to the graduating senior who most demonstrates living their life in harmony with body, mind, and spirit. That is so Ellen! Our family and her friends know this about her, but to have the school faculty recognize this was so gratifying.

For the next several years Ellen moved forward by working in the corporate world. When the devastating San Diego fires hit in 2003, Ellen had gone to the Qualcomm Stadium where evacuees were being sent. She knew she wanted to find some way to help. This led her to a job at a FEMA (Federal Emergency Management Agency) call center for the survivors of this disaster. Rather than needing to be rescued, Ellen had evolved into a role of helping others in need. She quickly moved up to a supervisor position and worked there for several months.

Her next employment was with Pfizer in Human Resources, and she enjoyed it so much she thought this might lead to a lifelong career. This position was not permanent, so she decided to take a position online where she trained employees of corporations like Best Buy and their Geek Squad in matters concerning customer service and new hire trainings.

Even while working full-time, Ellen continued to work with the other leaders in Impact Young Adults (IYA) to run the nonprofit. She and her organization started winning awards for their work with young adults with mental illness from the National Alliance on Mental Illness (NAMI), San Diego, and the California Bipolar Foundation.

As Ellen became a fully functioning adult, someone no longer defined by her bipolar diagnosis, our relationship as mother and daughter shifted. We spoke often and shared what was happening in our lives. We leaned on one another for support. We had become friends in addition to being family. I was deeply grateful for her healing and how she was able to not only live a "normal" life but an extraordinary one as well.

IYA kept doing outreach to bring in more members, all the while having fun activities every weekend. Local health and social service providers for young people with mental illness where contacted and asked for referrals of possible members. Having worked closely with NAMI, Ellen asked them to join with her. NAMI had helped her to see her ill-ness not as something that held her back, but as something that had given her experiences that would help her reach her goals.

After a few years of meeting weekly, Ellen and Johanna recognized the purpose of IYA was not just about social activities, it was about leadership training. Each member was getting an opportunity, if they chose, to plan and execute different activities that helped IYA function. Some members planned the activities while others became officers.

I visited Ellen almost every year after her college graduation. At one point, her roommate was Jennifer, one of the IYA members. When I first met the IYA group, it was obvious that each of them had challenges that kept them from being able to carry on a full conversation. Many of them seemed very shy and withdrawn, including Jennifer. In the few years since I had first met Jennifer, she had blossomed. She now had a job at Sea World whereas before she was not able to work because her symptoms were so severe. Now she was animated, using her hands when she talked, and she looked me straight in the eyes. Her own eyes sparkled with delight. She even had a boyfriend. Before long she started attending college and has a goal of becoming a Medical Social Worker.

I knew this organization was a way for young people with mental illness to find friends and help remove the social isolation they often experience, but I was amazed to wit-ness a member becoming a young adult living fully in all areas of life as a result of her involvement with the program. Despite all of Ellen's successes, her growth and her courage, the road is not always smooth for her, even today. As usually happens with people who have a BPD diagnosis, Ellen needs to have her medications readjusted at times when symptoms increase. When she is changing to a new medication, it can sometimes take weeks or even months for the new medicine to take effect. During this time period her symptoms can be debilitating. Her symptoms of depression can make it very difficult to work due to lack of concentration, inability to sleep, flu-like symptoms, and suicidal thoughts. In Ellen's case, she has been unable to work consistently and has had to go on disability assistance.

As Ellen's depression symptoms continued and she was unable to work, she wanted to go back to school and get her graduate degree to continue to prep herself for her career. She found an M.A. program through the University of San Diego called "Non-Profit Leadership and Management" and after a lot of thought and consideration, she applied. With over 100 applicants Ellen was one of 26 accepted into the program.

At first, she wondered if this was a good fit for her. It took a great deal of focus and commitment to keep pursuing her Master's degree. In 2010 she decided to take the summer off, instead of going year round her first year. This helped raise her spirits and she was placed with a new group of students she enjoyed working with.

IYA was chosen for a group course work project. Ellen found herself working with a group of dynamic leaders successful in their own non-profits who were now putting their energies into expanding the work of IYA. Ellen's plan is to spread IYA into northern San Diego County and eventually state and nationwide. Everyone who hears about the successes of IYA wants to see a chapter in their own community. This group in her Master's program helped her to create a Public Service Announcement (PSA) to reduce the stigma of mental illness on young adults. It's called "We Are MORE."(I.e., "We are MORE than our mental illness.") Her faculty counselor has said she will help Ellen find funding for this umbrella organization she is creating to help start more IYA-type groups. Her counselor has even told her the faculty wants her to consider getting her PhD at USD. Great work for a young woman who previously was so debilitated she could not get through one college class! It's easy for me to slip into the role of bragging mom, but how can I help my-self?

During her graduate studies, Ellen was also asked to sit on the Board of Directors of the International Bipolar Foundation (IBPF). The mission of this organization is to eliminate Bipolar Disorder through the advancement of research; to provide and enhance care and support services for all affected, and to erase associated stigma through public education. Ellen is contributing the leadership expertise that she has learned through her Master's program. In addition, this experience will help her lead the umbrella organization she is creating that will bring more IYA-type organizations to young people affected by mental illness.

The founder of the IBPF, Muffy Walker, called on leaders in politics and the entertainment industry to bring attention to their cause. Over the past few years through being on the Board, Ellen has been able to meet people like Glenn Close, the actress, whose sister, Jessie, has a diagnosis of Bipolar Disorder. Ms. Close spoke at an IBPF program put on to bring attention to the stigma and discrimination against those diagnosed with mental illness. IBPF has had speakers attend their events such as Margaret Trudeau, wife of the former Canadian Prime Minister Pierre Trudeau, Maurice Bernard, an actor on the daytime General Hospital series who in real life has BPD, and Patrick Kennedy, former US Congressman and son of the late Senator Ted Kennedy, where they have shared their experiences with BPD and have been honored for the work they are doing to further re-search and education. These experiences are taking Ellen into the world as a leader and will help her to find spokes-people for her organization that will bring even more light to the needs of young adults with mental illness.

The core message of Ellen's experience with BPD is that no matter what apparent obstacles you face, when you keep moving forward you will find strength by persisting through these challenges. As her mother, I experienced the pain of watching her succumb to debilitating depression and with it, the loss of the dreams I had for her life. I witnessed her despair in not being able to work toward her dreams. She showed me and all who knew her that if you keep moving ahead, you will reach your dreams. There are no limits to how far you can go. Ellen Frudakis is demonstrating this for me, for all the young people who are a part of Impact Young Adults, for anyone with a mental health diagnosis, and now you too, who know her story.

Even if you find yourself in a paralyzed state of emotion, a state of failure, or unable to see any possibility of living your dreams, take one step forward in creating them. This step will make all the difference in leading your life and your team to the success you've longed for.

Chapter Nine

*"The whole point of being alive is to evolve
into the complete person you were intended to be."*
– Oprah Winfrey

**Message Nine:
Find Clarity, Set Intentions and Attract Miracles**

Looking back on your life, have you made it all you want it to be?

Did you squeeze all the juiciness out of it and put the best of yourself out for you and all to enjoy?

Sometimes we swing out BIG to live our dreams and we fall flat on our face. But a wise anonymous person said this about failures: "Your past mistakes are meant to guide you, not define you." Even if you haven't evolved to a place where you are living the life of your dreams, use what you have learned to keep moving forward. In the movie, The Best Exotic Marigold Hotel, the proprietor, Sonny, proclaims no matter what obstacle he encounters, "Everything will turn out alright in the end and if it isn't alright, then it isn't the end."

I hired Bill Lamond as my coach after I attended the UN Conference on Women in Beijing, China, because I wanted to make a big impact in my world with what I experienced there. Bill taught me whatever I gave my focus to is what I would create. He said if I focused on what I didn't want, my mind would see this as what I wanted. He taught me how to focus my thinking "above the line." This line is an imaginary one with joy, pleasure, and fulfillment in life above it, and negativity, frustration and failure below. No matter what happened, he said I could always see things as "above the line. "This helped me to be clear about what I intended to manifest. Even when I have experienced events that I have not wanted, I have focused on finding the "gift" in the experience. Feeling my feelings from whatever life brings me, whether it is joy or pain, I have access to embracing all the richness my life experiences bring me. An example of this is when I am sick. I see it as perfect, that there is something I no longer need that is detoxifying from my body and preparing me to be more of who I came here to be. Here are a few ways to discover what you want from your life:

- Make a list of what you would love to have in your life. List what is nearest and dearest to your heart—no filtering! Keep a journal with this list and keep adding to it as things come up. Bill called this my "Appetites" or "Desires" list. Maybe you desire a new career, one that expresses who you really are, what you love to do, and where you can make the biggest impact. This way you'll never "work" another day because every action you take comes from truly living your passion. Maybe travel is one of your interests and you make a list of the places you want to visit. Perhaps spending more time at a hobby you love is one of your goals. Maybe it is getting healthier, or perhaps expanding your ability to receive love from others. As you focus on your own fulfillment, filling yourself up with your deepest desires, you naturally have

more to give to others. When you give from a place of fullness, there is a feeling of abundance for everyone involved. If you give from a place of lack or insufficiency, no one is really served.
- Meditate: ask Spirit to show you your highest and best outcome right now. If you find your higher power out in nature, go for a walking meditation.
- Ask your intuition what dream to focus your energies on now.
- Pick a divination card. Ask a question regarding what dream to focus on. I often pick from a variety of cards and highly recommend the Guiding Signs 101 cards created by Kathleen McIntire.
- Create an intention. Write it down. See it as already happening. FEEL it as if it is already done. Feeling is the magnet that will attract it into your life. It does not come to us from our minds. Let go of any attachment as to how it will come about.
- Listen for guidance. I often find that answers come to me through others. It is like they are messengers from my guides telling me the answers to the questions I have asked. I make a mental note that this is the answer I've been looking for.
- Sometimes the answers to your questions don't come right away, so just sit with it; sleep on it knowing it will be revealed to you in the right timing. When you are feeling doubtful about what actions to take in fulfilling your dreams, it is doubt that is mirrored back to you. It is important to not take action when in doubt; wait for the clarity. The more that you keep letting go of impatience to find that place of clarity, the faster and more precisely you draw your true purpose and action steps to you. It is

important to listen to your heart and soul and not what others think is best for you.

I am passionate about travel and was invited to go to Ecuador and visit the Amazon rainforest. Two of my dearest friends were co-leading a trip of women. We had an opportunity to live deep in the Amazon with the Achuar Indians who call the rainforest their home. I had all the desire to go, but no idea where the money would come from. It was 2009 and I had invested heavily in real estate prior to the real estate bubble burst. I had been attempting to sell these investments, but no one seemed to be buying anything, even at a deep discount. Getting the intuitive whisper that I was supposed to go on this trip, I filled out the application and sent in my deposit. I've always loved this Goethe quote about commitment:

"Until one is committed, there is hesitancy, the chance to draw back.
Concerning all acts of initiative (and creation),
there is one elementary truth
the ignorance of which kills countless ideas and splendid plans:
that the moment one definitely commits oneself,
then Providence moves too.
All sorts of things occur to help one
that would never otherwise have occurred.
A whole stream of events issues from the decision,
raising in one's favor all manner of unforeseen incidents
and meetings and material assistance,
which no man could have dreamed would have come his way.
Whatever you can do, or dream you can do, begin it.
Boldness has genius, power, and magic in it.
Begin it now."
–Johann Wolfgang von Goethe

The next day, I got a call about a piece of land that I'd had for sale for a year. The prospective buyer came right over. To my delight, he put an offer on it right there and then. Escrow was to close before I left on the trip. This was the sign I was looking for that I should go on this journey, and now I would have the means to pay for it.

On the trip to Ecuador, we visited an Achuar village deep in the Amazon rainforest. The only way to get there is by small plane landing on a dirt landing strip, then by long boat that meanders up the Capahuari River. We stayed in a thatched roof long house with no walls. Each of us had a space on the dirt floor covered with a straw mat and encased in a mosquito net to protect us from contracting malaria.

During the two days we spent with this village, we were shown the benefits of their culture. They have created a "dream culture" and believe their dreams are informing them how to live their lives. Each morning they awaken at dawn, drink Wayusa tea that purges and detoxifies their bodies, and then they sit in a circle and tell the dreams they experienced the night before.

We were allowed to experience a sacred ceremony that evening with the village Shaman, Don Miguel Ruiz. The Achuar do this ceremony regularly as a powerful way to connect deeply with Spirit and be given messages for their lives. We ingested a drink called Ayauasca, which is made from a vine and from a leaf from another plant that grow far apart in the jungle. We sat in a circle with the Shaman and spoke our intentions to the ceremony. I wanted more clarity regarding the work I am to do.

The Shaman blessed the space with his chanting, shaking of a plant rattle, and spitting alcohol laced with sweet and citrus aroma filled cologne called Florida Water. We came up one by one and took a drink of this thick, bitter tasting green plant concoction, then were led out to sit on banana leave out in the open dirt area, away from the long house. The sky was deep indigo and the stars were so bright. I had experienced Ayauasca before, but this time it was much different. I felt dizziness and ringing in my ears. People often have purging episodes. The vine drink is meant to detoxify the body so people often experience vomiting and diarrhea as a result. I had severe nausea, but no purging.

Eventually, I sunk into a place where I was shown something unbelievable. I had known from previous counseling that I had experienced sexual trauma as a pre-verbal child. This Shamanic experience confirmed the abuse. It wasn't emotional, but was very matter-of-factly revealed to me. I was also given the message that the abuse wasn't about me; it was a result of the abuser feeling angry about something and misplacing the anger towards me. I was able to completely let this experience go and experience healing. I didn't have to undergo years of therapy or carry the burden of this abuse any longer. I was able to forgive this person completely and move forward in my life.

This Shamanic healing continues to be one of the most powerful experiences of my life. I now see why I was called to commit to going on the trip, even though I didn't know where the money was coming from. I have no doubt why the money showed up so effortlessly. This experience, this healing was supposed to happen. I listen carefully whenever I feel a calling to do something and trust the universe to make arrangements. I am open to receive all that I am to have.

Sometimes we create something in our lives that seems like it will serve us forever, then life changes and our creation no longer serves us. I had always wanted to build a home. I enjoy construction and even though I didn't do any of the actual physical labor, I loved the collaboration with the contractor and his team. In 2005 I was able to fulfill this dream and the finished product turned into a sanctuary for my daughter and me. We so enjoyed living there.

At least, I did until my daughter grew up and moved out. This beautiful home was now too big for me. It was so expensive to heat and maintain. I ended up just living in my bedroom and heating it with its fireplace. Though difficult to imagine letting go of this beautiful home, it didn't fit my life anymore and I realized it was time to let it go.

Moving had always been difficult for me, so I chose to have this move to be different. As an expression of the joy I felt living there, I decided to create my leaving it just as enjoyable.

I felt a calling in November 2011, to make a move to San Diego. I wasn't sure where I would be living, so I desired to make moving there an adventure, to let go of everything I had except what would fit in my car. I could always buy new things to fit the new place I would call home. I gave my-self a year to complete the move.

I teamed up with my dear friend, Gracie, and we held a series of garage sales. I was able to sell most of the big items and a lot of the smaller ones. Other belongings were sold online. I had lived in that house for 8 years. It is amazing what a person can collect in that amount of time. Slowly the bedrooms and closets emptied out.

In August 2012, I put my home on the market. It was a short sale, as I built the house in 2005, just as the real estate bubble was about to pop. The market price when I listed the property for sale was two thirds of what it cost to build. There had been time to realize this was the case, so I was ready to let go and accept this, too. I would have more homes in my future. I kept telling myself the wise words of Sonny, "Everything always works out in the end."

The house had a cash offer quickly, but it took several months to complete the short sale with the bank. I kept letting go of more and more things. Finally, down to the last few weeks before I was to leave, I opened the multitude of cupboards spread throughout the house in the kitchen, utility room, and bathrooms. Oh my, why did I think I was al-most done letting go? I discovered that in one's cupboards lies the entire thing one doesn't want to deal with! So much stuff had been saved thinking I would someday use it but never did. Dear friends stepped in to help me clean them out. It was a beautiful community effort. I DID get to have my gracious leaving of this place I had adored creating and living in. I left with the house empty, except for the items the new buyer was purchasing, my car packed to the gills, and some boxes of memorabilia I left at my mother and my friend Amy's homes. I was off on to my next adventure.

On my way to San Diego, I attended Marianne Williamson's Sister Giant event in Los Angeles. At lunch the first day I met a woman named Melinda Pajak. I felt such a sisterhood with her as she had written a book and called her-self the Intention Master. She was a woman who believed in manifesting dreams—her own and other's. We got to know one another over the weekend and she invited me to attend a Moon Class put on by one of her spiritual teachers Beatrex Quntanna, in San Diego. The first week I landed in San Diego, I went to the class and felt an immediate connection to Beatrex and the class attendees. I felt as though I had been guided to the perfect community for me.

During the next few weeks more synchronicities occurred. I received an email regarding a publishing and marketing mentor, John Eggen of Mission Publishing and Marketing, who could help me complete, publish, and market this book? After creating this book for six years, through working with him I was able to publish it in nine months.

I wanted to create a new career… speaking, writing, teaching workshops, and coaching others in living their dreams. I received another email a week later and found another marketing expert to help me build my coaching practice. The miracles kept unfolding and I was drawing the perfect support to living the life I had wanted for so long.

I was looking for a place to live that was peaceful and nurturing for me to complete my book. Again, thanks to Melinda, I was led to a beautiful wildlife sanctuary that was built to honor the Divine Feminine, and was able to complete my manuscript in an environment where hawks and ravens soared above, hummingbirds flitted about, coyotes roamed, and bunnies and ground squirrels scurried. Besides that, it deeply nourished my soul. As I was completing writing, I was called to have it focus on what my true calling in my life is; to call forth the wisdom and leadership of women in our world.

I had seen it just happen for me. By listening (and heeding) the call to come to San Diego even though I didn't completely understand why, clarity was present for me to fulfill my deepest dream.

When you follow your calling and your heart's desire with clarity, what you need lines up for you. It isn't about having everything; it is about attracting exactly what you need and desire in that moment. Amazingly, doors open effortlessly and real magic happens when you simply allow things to come your way.

What do you want to create and manifest in your life? Write your vision, goals and intentions down. See them as

already here. Open up to miracles. Allow yourself to receive all the good that wants to come to you.

Chapter Ten

*"Magic is believing in yourself,
if you can do that, you can make anything happen."*

– Johann Wolfgang von Goethe

**Message Ten:
Believe in yourself and your dreams**

In 2005, just after I moved into the home I had built, I heard about a principle called Masterminding, which is a goal-achievement tradition practiced by luminaries like Ben Franklin and Henry Ford. It's the practice where like-minded individuals meet regularly to support each other's progress toward similar intentions and goals. I was familiar with Napoleon Hill's book **Think and Grow Rich** and how he believed our thinking and connecting with Divine thinking can be used to create anything we want in our lives. I believed that too.

I asked a roommate and some friends in a Toastmasters club we all belonged to if they would like to create a Mastermind group. At the time, I was working as a realtor and with three other powerful women working with me, I felt certain I could create my dreams and live the life I desired. I wanted to believe more in myself and I felt by partnering with them, it would not only help me, but them too.

We worked together for a year. Two of the women ended up moving out of the area as a result of creating and living their dreams. My roommate and I assembled another group of friends. This group didn't have the necessary commitment and eventually disbanded.

My dear friend Robin Milam and I kept looking for a woman to form another Mastermind group. We learned from the previous group's lack of success that we really needed to find the right woman to join us this time. At a Gather the Women meeting in Nevada City in April 2007, we found a match. Her name is Kathleen McIntire. At the meeting she spoke about her intention to bring the Divine feminine energy more fully into our world. Her process was to bring women together for ritual work. I had also brought women together for rituals so I felt an immediate connection to her. Robin and I signed up for her ritual group.

Soon thereafter, Robin and I invited Kathleen to lunch at The New Moon restaurant in Nevada City and shared this idea with her. She was thrilled and we chose a date to begin meeting.

We rotated meeting at one of our homes. As we joined hands and read the Mastermind principles that asked us to surrender ordinary thinking, focus the power of intention to be open to all possibilities, that through the power of our group our dreams and desires would naturally be created, a new bond formed between us. Even though the principles speak Mastermind, it was clear to us that this is Spirit, the ever present source, the creator/creatrix that is love, light, pure intelligence, and powerful beyond measure that was working through us to create without limitation. This was the source we were tapping into.

We did a three-step process every time we met:

• The first step was to check-in and share what was happening in each one's life. Listening was the job of the other two, really listening with an open heart and not interrupting the person sharing.

• The second step was asking for coaching or advice on the intention each was working on. Sometimes a member would use this time for more check-in. It is amazing how when you have someone to deeply listen you can figure out what steps to take on your own. This is part of the magic of this process.

• The third step was to "see" one another having brought our intentions into our lives, to see each of us actually living our dream. The job of the person being seen was to not interrupt, but to truly "take in" and "receive" what the "seers" were saying to them. Here's an example:

"Robin, I see your organization, Rights of Mother Nature, flourishing and that you easily have 1,000,000 people sign the Declaration of the Rights of Mother Nature so that you can present the signatures to the leader-ship of the Rio 20 UN Conference on the Environment. I see you having more income as you build this organization, so that there is funding for everything the organization and you need. I also see you and Tom (her husband) going on a fun vacation this year."

At first we timed ourselves so we would complete the process in 90 minutes. Sometimes one of us would have more to say so we would adjust accordingly. We wanted each person to have enough time to communicate, but eventually we ended up intuitively knowing how much time we could take. This process worked every time.

At the beginning we scheduled meeting every two weeks. There were times when travel or other scheduling forced us to meet once a month, but we had our best results when we met every two weeks. We soon realized the name, Mastermind, didn't fit us. We are three hearts -centered women, so we named ourselves the Heart Triad. Amazing things have happened since we started meeting:

Robin created an Internet marketing business, but found it wasn't her true calling. In our current group, she followed her passion to preserve the Rights of Mother Nature. She was hired to be the administrator of The Global Alliance for the Rights of Mother Nature. Here is what she says about the value of our Heart Triad in her life:

> "Our triad is, and has been, a powerful anchoring rod. The last five to six years have been a time of significant transition, especially as I learn to follow my heart's deepest desire to engage fully in work that is deeply aligned with my passion –to become a global advocate for Rights of Nature and focusing on creating a future for generations to come. The deep listening we share and the sacred reaffirmation that occurs in our seeing of each other is vital. Our triad reaffirms my own listening to my inner voice and quiets my inner critic."

Kathleen created a healing sanctuary on her property; a divination card set called Guiding Signs 101 Cards, participates regularly with the Women's Nobel Peace prize group, and produced a film called "Mayan Renaissance." Here's what she said about our Heart Triad:

"In the five years Mary Elizabeth, Robin, and I have joined in our heart triad, there have been so many blessings. It is joyful beyond words to describe what it is like to have two conscious, brilliant, impeccable women love and hold my dreams and I in the highest and best way for me.

For 22 years I had been in a marriage where I was a satellite making my husband's dreams a reality and forgetting me. It was time for me to share the deepest essence of which I am—the parts of me who heal and channel Mother Mary and are mystical. My husband wanted those parts gone, so I left.

I came together with the heart triad about two years later. I was already leading rituals and ceremonies with women, and was transforming my 28 acres into a retreat center for birthing the new paradigm, a world of love that works for all life on our planet.

I lead sacred journeys for women. Once a year we go to places like the rainforest with the Achuar Tribe in Ecuador, to Guatemala around the Tzolkin–The Sacred Mayan calendar, or to sacred sites in Peru. These trips are about the sacred sites within us as well as on the land and an activation of remembering.

I created two websites:

www.SoaringInLight.com helps people with this huge shift of consciousness we are living in today. It is about bringing forward the voices of the feminine that have been suppressed, bringing forward the Divine Feminine wisdom on our planet.

www.GuidingSigns101.com highlights the Guiding Signs 101 Divination cards to help people access their own inner intuition and remember the place of power lies within us and not on the outside. The cards create authentic connection when used with other people.

I produced two Mayan films: *"Mayan Renaissance"* and *"Guatemaya, The Unification of Wisdom."* These films educate audiences in the wisdom from indigenous Maya people.

To me the word accomplishment implies something you have done. And as we are moving into a new era on our planet, the message I got was to slow down to the speed of being. I don't think it is possible to go forward into this new consciousness with the mindset we lived in before. And this new consciousness is why I have come to this planet. So I have been in the mystery of what is next for me for a few months now and getting in touch with the essence of my soul, finding direction in what truly is my deepest calling. Mary Elizabeth and Robin are amazing supports to me as I go through this next shift."

For **myself**, this heart triad supported me through some of the most challenging times of my life. I changed careers from real estate back to nursing and became a Hospice Nurse. I got in touch with the long-held dream to write a book and our triad even went to writing classes together. This triad helped me through moving to San Diego and starting my new life here. I attribute my writing, coaching, speaking, and teaching career to be a result of this heart triad. Its how I am creating the life I've always wanted. Even though I live at the other end of the state, we continue to meet via Skype and support our lives as they unfold and demonstrate the truth of what we came here to create.

We agree that the "seeing" is the most powerful part of the process. Here is what Kathleen says:

> "To me the "seeing" we do with each other is the most powerful gift there is. So often we have had parents, spouses, and a society that wants us to be different than we are. When we were younger, we often gave up our deepest essence to fit in and be accepted. I know I did and that was painful. To be seen for and as you truly are and seen in your highest potential of your calling and life dreams is what we all most long for and need. Each time I receive a "seeing" from my triad partners, it feels like the best birthday present in the world. It touches my heart and soul and inspires me. Another gift of being seen by others is that we often can't see our own greatest gifts that are so obvious to everyone else."

When I hear my heart triad sisters speak back to me what I have told them I want in my life, I am able to take in the truer possibility of it occurring. That little voice in your mind that says "Oh, THAT will never happen…it is just a pie in the sky dream" is quieted, and precious dreams like completing my book or getting paid for what I am passionate about feels real. I start telling myself I can do this. Their voices help me strengthen my own internal voice of encouragement.

As we continued to meet regularly and we collectively believed that our world needed more of the feminine, collaborative style of leadership brought forward, we wanted to share this process with more women. We felt our relationships with each other had become so deep through this process that we wanted to share it with others.

Our dream came true of sharing this with other women in September 2012 when we led a workshop called "Girl-friends Unite! Live Your Life Purpose with the Support of Your BFF'S" at our local Passion into Action women's conference put on by See Jane Do. The women who attended saw the power that was available through this process for creating their dreams.

Creating the life you want for yourself requires you to become a leader, to lead yourself into this new life. It requires believing in yourself and your dreams like never before. The great thing is you don't have to do it alone. There is strength and a sense of magic when you create together with like-minded women. Find two or more women you would love to start this process with, follow these steps, and you will be amazed at how miracles start showing up in your life.

Chapter Eleven

"Challenge is a dragon with a gift in its mouth. Tame the dragon and the gift is yours."

– Noela Evans

Love the Challenges: Give Gratitude and Appreciation for Everything and THRIVE!

There is no better way to tame the dragon, or all of the challenges we face as leaders, as individuals or as a collective society, than with gratitude. No matter how great the challenge is, there is always some benefit partnered with it. How many times does a tragic occurrence happen like a cri-sis in nature, a hurricane, earthquake, or tsunami, and the greatest gift is the way people come together to help their fellow man? Humanity seems to be wired this way.

But what if it is you who lost your home, either by an act of nature or through the housing bubble burst and securitization failure by the lending institutions in 2008? Do you love those dragons? I lost real estate in that crisis, but a mentor said to me: "When you invest in real estate, either you make money or you learn something." I am grateful for the knowledge I gained.

As Melanie Beattie says, "Gratitude unlocks the fullness of life. It turns what we have into enough, and more. It turns denial into acceptance, chaos into order, and confusion to clarity. It can turn a meal into a feast, a house into a home, a stranger into a friend." If you make friends with the challenges, the losses and the difficulties in your life, there is nothing you can't accomplish, especially living your dreams.

One of my dearest friends lost her home in a fire. Gracie MacKenzie said this about how, in spite of this tragedy, she learned to love her challenges:

"I lost most of my worldly wealth and possessions to a series of disasters in Costa Rica, ending with a raging fire in which my dream literally went up in smoke. Initially there was the trauma of it to deal with, which I survived by going to be with people who love me and would treat me with kindness and compassion. I followed the love. And I just kept consciously reminding myself that all of this is an illusion; that what really matters is the life of the soul, the love one has and gives away, and the ability to choose one's own beliefs and perceptions. I asked for help and friends gave money and shelter and clothes.

My son negotiated a car for me that I could pay for over time. I practiced gratitude so that I could stay focused on the good. It wasn't easy, but I could always say, 'Well, at least I have my health.'

And then the joints in my hands began to swell and hurt, and the words 'Osteoarthritis' and 'permanent' began to appear regularly in conversation. I became deeply fatigued and depressed, and for the first time in my life I couldn't sleep. I could no longer claim to be grateful for my health. Still, I couldn't help but notice each day that I was still here and giving up did not seem to be an option. I mean try it on: you give up. Then what? You either take on a life of feeling sorry for yourself (tried that when I was younger—no fun), or you keep going. So I kept going. Three things helped and were the stable tripod on which I reclaimed my life and rebuilt a new dream

The first, as I said before, was kind friends and family. One dear girlfriend in particular, the author of this book, has a gift for seeing and encouraging the best in people. She never chastised me for how I was feeling, but always pointed out the good that I was not able to see in the moment. She, my sister and others, lifted me up by assuring me that I am loved and cared for, and reminding me who I am as an infinite, creative, and beautiful person.

The second was my knowing and willingness to re-member what I had learned: that everything is subject to interpretation and I had a choice from moment to moment about mine; that the creativity of Spirit is infinite and is available to me here and right now, regard-less of appearance, and that I had survived worse than physical losses. I kept focusing on Spirit and asking what it wanted from me and for me, and listening for the guidance.

Thirdly, I returned to my Spiritual Community, the Sierra Center for Spiritual Living, which is a Science of Mind Church and teaches the principles that would support me in choosing and focusing on the thoughts and interpretations that could form the foundation on which a new life could be built.

In short, I surrounded myself with loving people whose very presence would hold me up until I regained my footing. It took about three years. I was diagnosed with a pre-verbal Post Traumatic Stress Disorder (PTSD) which helped immensely. Understanding that there was a known pattern, symptoms, and treatment for this mental imbalance caused by early childhood traumas was the opening to healing it. The loving sup-port of friends, family, and Spiritual community provided the ongoing reminders and sustenance for the work. The willingness to do the work—which was intense and difficult, was also key.

The soul is amazing, and if you can tap into yours, it can give you everything you need to move forward, even when you feel that you can't or that there's nothing to move forward towards. It says, "So what? Just do it because you can." At one point, mine said to me:
"This is what I've brought you here to do. All of this. So that you can know compassion in a deep and profound way. That is your gift. Why resist it for even a second?" That made me laugh. A lot of things made me laugh when I was in between dreams, and the best dream I could muster was that I would somehow get through this to a better time.

The soul is a dream factory. It will always give you a new dream if you spend time in silence and ask in earnest. Rising from the ashes on the wings of willing-ness, love, support, friends, community, and faith, I've been able to create a new dream. Inspired by friends and my own courageous self, I am beginning a book and recording some of my own songs to make my first solo CD. Whether I accomplish these things or not is not the most important thing. What's important is that I have the vision and allow it to call me forward on the path of my life, trusting that where it leads me is where I need to be.

I am 61 and unstoppable. Because I know that I get to choose, and I know that I am not alone. I have the inner willingness and courage, the power of Spirit, and the outer support of those with whom I am connected at the heart. What more could a person ask of life?"

Loving the challenges has taken me awhile, but the more I have had gratitude and appreciation for the gifts I've received from all of my challenges; the more I have been able to love them. What gifts have I received?

I can make it through ANY challenge.

I've experienced difficult childbirths, the death of my husband, being widowed at a young age, childhood trauma, and divorce at a young age, single parenthood, and children diagnosed with mental illness, loss of wealth, and been a Hospice nurse. Wow! I have made it through a lot and it hasn't dampened my spirits. I still look forward to a long, happy life.

I can stay grounded and fully on purpose, no matter what crisis or tragedy comes my way.

Even when my husband was going through cancer treatment and my daughter was in a locked mental facility, I stayed grounded and listened for what the next right action was.

I have developed an inner knowing and intuition of what is needed for me and those I care about to thrive.

When your loved ones have a chronic health issue, it is important to be a good advocate for them. The medical sys-tem we have now that is focused on illness instead of well-ness demands that we take responsibility for ourselves and our loved one's care. Get all the information you can to make the best decisions for their care and for your needs as a caregiver. I learned and my loved ones have learned to sit with the information gathered and listen for inner guidance be-fore taking action.

I speak my truth, which is spoken for the benefit of all involved, no matter what the situation.
The challenges I've faced have helped me know myself better, what is important to me, and how I want to live my life. They have taught me to respect mine and other's needs. If a situation doesn't honor others, or me I speak my truth.

I have not let my challenges make me bitter; I live with kindness in my heart.
My grandmother modeled this for me. She lost her husband at a young age and didn't remarry. She lived with a smile on her face and kindness in her heart. I was so blessed to have her as a mentor.

I have become intentional with my own self-care.
Even when it was painful to separate from my husband when he was in remission from cancer, and then to take a three-day break from care giving when he was dying, I knew I needed some rest and personal space to be able to live a balanced life. I believe this has kept me healthy and living in integrity with my own life needs.

I live my life with grace and flow, like running water.
I lived so many years resisting how my life had turned out. I was gracious with others, but not always with myself. As I developed more self-awareness and self-acceptance, I've learned to live my life by being in the flow. Change is inevitable and I've learned to be more flexible with the changes.

I feel my feelings and this keeps my heart open.
I have recently obtained this gift. Like so many people in our culture, I adopted the masculine way of stuffing my feelings. This led to a cycle of unhealthy coping patterns including overeating and drinking. As I engaged in these patterns, this led to feelings of anxiety, stress from guilt and remorse over the overeating and drinking which led to a vicious cycle. As I've let myself feel whatever emotions I am experiencing, the unhealthy coping skills have fallen away. I believe meditation, simplifying my life, and staying present in the moment allows me to stay current with my feelings as they arise. A benefit from this is that I am feeling so much more joy and aliveness.

With an open heart, I stay true to my purpose, which is creating a world that honors all life.
There are so many opportunities to be cynical about life, to adopt a way of thinking that life is always going to be difficult, or hard, or never allow for dreams to be fulfilled.

There is so much proof that life's problems can never be overcome: there may always be world hunger, war, bigotry, inequality between the genders, inhumane crime, and environmental degradation, but I believe it is still possible with the commitment of a critical mass of people to overcome life's greatest challenges. We have entered a turning of the ages where I believe it has never been more possible to create a world that honors all life.

I appreciate all the good in my life, for what I appreciate, expands.
It is not difficult to create a long list of things to be grateful for if you are living in the United States of America. We live in

a country of immense freedom and abundance, but I am especially grateful for those unexpected blessings that come my way out of nowhere: the person who smiles at you on the street; the hummingbird that flies up close to your face; a dog that leans into you when you pet it, or the beauty of a sunset. The more I notice the little things; I seem to at-tract even more to appreciate.

I take time to expand my knowledge and skills and this expands my appreciation for life and my ability to con-tribute to others.
I've made lifelong learning a part of my lifestyle. I've at-tended trainings, workshops, webinars, and teleconferences, have gone on spiritual journeys for shaman healings, and studied spiritual teachings. I love personal growth and will be doing it as long as I live. The knowledge and experiences I have gained have enriched my life and brought me to a place of wanting to share what I have learned to assist others in their own transformation.

I accept and appreciate myself exactly the way I am.
This is a gift I am giving myself this year. I have turned the corner from self-judgment and in accepting myself; I will be less judgmental of others. Love is the greatest gift I have to give others and myself.

I knew I had some unfinished business back at the beach in San Clemente where I almost drowned and this book began. Just before dawn on a clear January day in 2013, I re-traced my steps. I'm not entirely certain if I was on the same beach, but it really didn't matter. I felt compelled to go back there and see if there were any more gifts from the dragon I had encountered there.

The sun peeked over the cliffs on the opposite side of the train tracks as I walked south on the deserted beach. One train came by… then another. My father loved trains,

So whenever I see one, I feel his presence. I sensed the spot where it happened was about a mile down the shoreline. As I made this trek, fifty years after being caught in the riptide as an eight year old, fighting with everything I had to stay alive, the tears came. I cried for that little girl in me who couldn't cry that day.

As I got closer, I noticed how calm Grandmother Ocean was. There was a white lifeboat next to a sign that said "Beach Warning ~ Dangerous Riptides ~No Lifeguard on Duty ~Swimming Hazardous." The boat represented that I was saved that day, but my lifeboat wasn't a physical one.

A large sea plant that had washed up on the shore marked the place. She represented that brave child in me and was almost in the shape of a heart. I thanked her for everything she did to stay alive that day. I plucked a small green stone from her mass.

I made an altar and put the green stone on the right, a feather in the middle and a white stone on the left. The green stone represented my power. The feather stood for Spirit who commanded, "This is not the way you will die." The white stone was for all the angels and guides who were with me that day. I thanked them for their protection and helping me live. I forgave my brothers for ridiculing me; they were young boys who didn't comprehend what I had gone through out there with the dragon riptide. I forgave all men who have hurt me. I forgave myself for becoming a victim that day.

A new wave of peace and power washed over me. As I walked back down the beach, I found sweet purple flowers blooming, even in the middle of January. The flowers represented the new life blooming in me.

A final train came by; a new journey began. There was the bright blue clear sky above—a blank canvas to create new life on. When you complete the past and find the gifts in your challenges, there is nothing but possibility available for you to create the life of your dreams. These experiences teach us what we need to know to live the life we've always wanted for ourselves.

Now is the time. Write down the life you've always wanted to live. People who write down their goals, share them with a friend, then send an update to that friend every week are 33% more successful in achieving their goals. Put this vision up where you can see it and read it every day. Picture yourself living life just the way you like it to be. Feel what it is like to have the career you want, the family experiences, the travel, and the difference you'd like to make in other people's life. Let those feelings soak down deep, breathe them in, and appreciate Spirit for bringing you this life of your dreams. Hold them as if they have already happened. You can have this! As you lead yourself to the life of your dreams, your deepest heart's desires, you will lead and inspire others.

Like nature, we are meant to thrive.

Each of us can live a life where we are thriving and living the life of our dreams. All you do is really desire your dreams, line up your actions, and let go of limited thinking. Sounds simple, doesn't it?

So why aren't we all living the life of our dreams? Are you saying to yourself?

- I don't have the time…

- I don't have the energy…
- I will once the kids grow up…
- I'm a single parent to my children. How can I do what I really want with my life now?
- As soon as I finish (the dishes, cleaning my closet, paying off my credit cards, paying off my student loan), I'll get right on that…
- Oh, I would, but I need to develop more skills in that area so after I go to school…After I clean out the junk drawer…
- I just need to get that remodeling project done…
- I don't have enough money to start a new business
- My wife/husband/partner is going back to school, so when he/she is done with that…
- I need to make enough money to live on so how can I do what I really want to be doing?

Do these statements sound familiar? They do to me because these are some of the things that I've told myself. These messages may sound true, but they really aren't. They are limiting beliefs we adopted. We think these beliefs are written in stone and cannot be changed or even looked at, but the truth is they are just decisions or choices we made.

When my second daughter was 3 years old I said I wanted to be a speaker and a coach for people wanting to live their dreams and become change-makers, and I wanted to write and publish a book. She is now twenty years old! The good thing is it is never too late to live your dreams. It is never too late to change limiting beliefs. It is never too late to make new choices in life. Life is constantly changing and the changes in our world are calling for us to lead.

What if you decided to be in charge of the changes, to chart your own course, to create life just the way you want it.

It's true that some people can do this by themselves. I think we've all heard of the "pull yourself up by your boot-straps" model. But for most of us, it is so much faster and easier to have a partner, a committed partner to help us, one who wants you to achieve your dreams, to live your life in line with what you value, to have the results you want in your life.

Maybe you:

- Work a 9-5 job, but you have a business idea you always wanted to create, one that will make an impact not only in your life, but has a ripple effect out into the world.
- Know a solution to a problem that affects many, but never put it into an action plan
- Work in the mail room but secretly want the corner office and to lead from your own natural, authentic leadership style.
- Always knew you had a book in you, one that could impact so many people's lives.
- Were told you could never make a living from your dream, but that is all you've ever wanted to do and you know if lived this dream, it would make such a difference to so many.

Whatever your dream or vision is, you will find the support from my programs and services. Here is how I can assist you in this quest:

- **Join the Wise and Ready to Rise IMPACT Training**. Take this six-week teleconference training where you will learn effective ways to take your vision from a dream to a reality. www.WiseaAndReadyToRise.com

- **Leadership Coaching.** I work with a limited number of clients one-on-one to achieve their leadership goals and dreams. Go to my website www.WiseAnd Ready-ToRise.com and sign up for a complimentary consultation to create a vision for your life and a plan that will have you living this vision now. A member of my team will contact you to set up an appointment.
- **Live Events.** I host regular live events where you will experience the transformation of your dream and vision becoming real. You'll meet other partners to help you on your path and be expanded in your leadership capacity. Go to www.WiseAndReadyToRise.com and subscribe to my newsletter for schedules.
- **Speaking.** I am available to share my uplifting message with your company, conference, or organization.

Ask for details on my website and a member of my team will contact you.

You can make it through any challenge, harvest the gifts from it, and keep moving forward to create your dreams no matter what happens in your life. You have all the resources within you to make this happen, to be open to all the good that wants to come your way, and to believe in yourself and your dreams to have the life you have always wanted, to create the world you have always wanted.

I am here to inspire you to create and live your vision. You are not alone. There are seen and unseen sources working to bring about your vision. Let's start creating what you came to earth to experience. Go to www.wiseandready-torise.com and let's bring forth your life as you were meant to live it.

The words of Marianne Williamson say it best:

"Our deepest fear is not that we are inadequate. Our deepest fear is that we are powerful beyond measure. It is our light, not our darkness that most frightens us. We ask ourselves, who am I to be brilliant, gorgeous, talented, and fabulous? Actually, who are you not to be? You are a child of GOD. You're playing small does not serve the world. There is nothing enlightened about shrinking so that other people won't feel insecure around you. We are all meant to shine, as children do. We were born to make manifest the glory of God that is within us. It's not just in some of us; it's in every-one. And as we let our own light shine, we unconsciously give other people permission to do the same. As we are liberated from our own fear, our presence automatically liberates others."

Let's liberate your talents, inspire you to claim your vision, and have you live the life you were meant to live; to make the contribution of your gifts to the world. Let's Thrive!

About the Author

Mary Elizabeth Young discovered her strengths as a leader through challenging circumstances. Her two daughters had mental health diagnoses and her beloved husband faced a terminal illness and died at a young age. The courage she gained from these experiences fueled her desire to live a fulfilling life no matter what challenges came her way, and compelled her to keep moving forward, to dream big and manifest miracles.

As CEO of her family's geotechnical engineering business, Mary Elizabeth directed the firm as they partnered with ATT, Sprint, and Nextel to construct the network framework for cellular technology to expand throughout California.

As an activist for women, she attended the UN Conference on Women in Beijing, China, and returned to her com-munity to co-found a women's leadership organization, Gather the Women in Nevada County, CA.

As a visionary, she participated in global social change organizations such as The Hunger Project, The Pachamama Alliance, Women's Earth Alliance, and Pioneer's. She is committed to creating a world that works for all life.

As a mother and a certified Hospice and Palliative Care RN, she leads from her heart, knowing that compassion is the universal language that connects us all.

She inspires audiences to see the gifts in their challenges and use them as the fuel to create the life of their dreams. People who attend her workshops say they generate a clear vision for their hopes and aspirations, and form a plan for how to realize them.

This book, **Wise and *Ready* to Rise**, demonstrates, especially to women, that life has taught them natural leadership qualities. She encourages women to step up and lead NOW, just in time as our world is calling us to be the change that makes a difference for all.

Made in the USA
Middletown, DE
08 September 2020